LESSONS FOR LIFE

Lessons for Life

ROBERT I. KAHN

Doubleday & Company, Inc.

GARDEN CITY, NEW YORK

1963

Grateful acknowledgment is hereby made to Station KPRC, Houston, Texas, for permission to incorporate in this book some material previously used in my sermonettes broadcast by that station, and to the Houston *Chronicle* for permission to adapt material from my weekly column, "Lessons for Life."

TO MY FAMILY

My parents, who nurtured body, mind, and soul.
My wife, partner of my heart.
Our children, in whom are our hopes.

Contents

I

Living with God

1

If You Want to Improve, Take a Lesson

I was given my first golf clubs at the age of twelve and began to "duffer" around the course with a boy friend every Sunday for years. My game improved little by little. Before long I was even hitting the ball! And the time came when I broke a hundred. That was a day! But then I improved no more.

My friend made progress at about the same rate, but after he had broken a hundred, he continued to improve until he was shooting in the high eighties. I could not understand it. We were about the same age. He was no more of a natural athlete than I, and yet his golf game improved and mine did not. In an effort to overtake him, I began to practice my game after school. But it did no good. My game did not improve. And so finally in envious exasperation, I asked him how he manged to improve his golf. His answer was simple: "I take lessons."

That night I asked my father, who had been quite an athlete in his youth, what difference it made. "I practice," I said, "and everyone says that practice makes perfect."

I have never forgotten my father's reply. "Practice will only make perfect if the practice is directed to perfection. You are practicing without supervision, without understanding what it is you are trying to do. You may be holding the club wrong, swinging back wrong, using your wrists wrong, and all that practice does is to perfect your faults! If you want to improve, take a lesson and then practice what you have learned."

In the years since, I have had occasion to remember those words many times. Many of our efforts to live well are frustrated because we try to "go it alone," to learn from just our own experience, when all the time there is the cumulative moral wisdom of the race available to us. As a pastor, I see this again and again in the religious doubts of young people, in the frustrations of family happiness, in the area of personal relations. It is not that people will not work at life; they work hard, they practice continually, but their life-score fails to improve because they do not take lessons; they seem reluctant to turn to the past for spiritual guidance.

It is, of course, a remarkable thing that we should still turn to the past for spiritual guidance; that even in a world in which technology is racing into the future with supersonic speed, morality should still be expressed in Biblical formulations.

This would seem to be a paradox. We do not turn to the Bible for our knowledge of agriculture; we do not search it for chemical or physical scientific knowledge; we do not depend on the Bible for our military tactics or weapons (although it would be something of a privilege to live once again in a world in which the deadliest weapon was a spear or sword), but we do turn to it for our faith, our religion, our way of life.

And while some might suggest that we have outgrown the old-time religion, and need a new faith and a new morality, the plain fact of the matter is that we have yet to catch up with the Bible's ideals. The Ten Commandments will not be obsolete until men stop lying and stealing and murdering, both as individuals and as nations; the law of brotherly love is still as absolute an ideal as it was three thousand years ago.

These lessons for life, therefore, lean heavily upon tradition, upon the literature of the Bible, upon the teachings of the Talmud, which is the post-Biblical development of Jewish thought and morality, upon the various writings of the Jewish religious past.

The insights of Moses and the prophets, of psalmists and philosophers help us see our own lives against the moral guideposts of history, and help us solve our contemporary problems by eternal truths.

Faith makes a difference

Our whole life, and the life of mankind, depends on our faith. Our fate, and the fate of the world, hangs on what we believe.

Many people find this difficult to accept. One friend of mine was holding forth on the general subject of religion. "It doesn't make any difference what a man believes," he said. "What makes a difference is what he does. I do not judge a man by his doctrines, I judge him by his behavior."

In one way my friend is right. We see too many people whose beliefs and actions fail to square themselves. They say they believe one thing, and behave as though they believe another. But hypocrisy does not invalidate the truth that what men believe, sincerely believe, is vitally important to their lives and the life of society. Wrong principles lead to wrong actions. A man's doctrine, faith, theology, philosophy, call it whatever you will, is the foundation of his character, and a people's values determine a people's history. Faith is the foundation of our ethical systems, faith is the compass for our moral direction, faith sets the goal of our spiritual ambition. Our life, and the life of mankind, depends on our faith.

First of all, what we believe is the foundation of our ethics. For analogy we might turn to geometry. On the first few pages of a geometry textbook there are listed a few axioms, or self-evident truths. "A straight line is the shortest distance between two points." "Things equal to the same thing are equal to each other," and so forth. The book then goes on to build upon these axiomatic foundations a series of more and more complicated geometric theorems. The end of the book is contained in its page of axioms.

More than this, the principles derived from the axioms are useful; they help men to build bridges, erect skyscrapers, dig oil wells.

But let anyone overlook or ignore an axiom, the theorem will be faulty, the bridge will collapse. The self-evident truths are the foundation.

So it is with what a man believes and what he does. Start with a few simple propositions, with a set of fundamental beliefs, and you can build upon them an ethical system that will point the way of right and wrong in every avenue of life. But take away an article of faith or change it, and you will have an ethics that has no foundation and cannot endure.

For example, for a long time men believed, or were taught to believe, in the divine right of kings. Kings were not kings by popular assent, they were kings by the appointment of God. Therefore, men dared not revolt against them, speak ill of them, nor even question their right to be kings. God created royalty, let men obey without question. This was the axiom underlying absolute monarchy.

Today, we subscribe to a different set of axioms. "We hold *these* truths to be self-evident . . . that all men are created equal." And with a change of belief, we have seen a change of government. No longer will we tolerate absolute monarchs who claim to rule by the grace of God. All men are endowed by God with certain inalienable rights. No man has the right to rule over his fellow man without that man's consent. No man can stand up and say: "God has appointed me as your ruler."

Or, to take another example, a simple axiom such as the greatest good for the greatest number leads us to the practice of majority rule. Yet, this axiom alone can lead to the abuse of minorities, to the slaughter of Huguenots, or to the liquidation of kulaks. But if we add another axiom, the inalienable rights of men, then we preserve the majority's right to rule and the minority's right to protection from the abuse of majority power.

Would you still say that what a man believes makes no difference? It makes a great difference because men act upon their convictions and order their society on the foundation of their faith.

To be strong or to be kind

What a man believes is vitally important in the second place because faith is a compass for rediscovering moral directions. Almost every choice we have in life, almost every problem we face, almost every dilemma that troubles us, can only be solved by taking our moral bearings, by examining the problem in the light of our beliefs about the nature and purpose of life.

Take, for example, the issue of civil rights. This, one of our most perplexing social problems, is not merely a question of states' rights against federal usurpation of power, nor a struggle between North and South, nor of big-city Democratic machines against countryside Democrats. It involves, actually, the problem of what we believe. If we believe that God has created superior races and inferior races, then we arrive at one answer. If, on the other hand, we believe that *all* men are children of God, and equal in the sight of God, then we come out with another answer. Differences in the program and our thinking about the program are the results of differences in belief.

Or, if we turn to the subject of philanthropy and ask, "What is my responsibility to my fellow man—how much should I give to the United Fund, or why should I support the Goodwill Industries?" we are immediately involved in deeper questions of faith. Not every civilization has tried to help its helpless. Spartans put their babies out on the hillsides so that only the strong would survive. Certain Pacific islanders, I am told, force their aging to climb a palm tree once each year, and then shake the tree to rid themselves of those no longer able to support themselves. And some anthropologists, like the late Earnest Hooton, claim we are coddling the weak and thereby weakening the race. Why, then, should we care for the weak, the helpless, the disabled? The only answer is in our theology. Is the purpose of life to be strong, or is the purpose of life to be kind?

Conditions in our jails and reformatories and penitentiaries are also problems of faith. If we believe that God wants us to take revenge on those who break the law, then the worse our jails are, the better they serve this purpose. But if we believe that vengeance belongs to God, then our penal system will be designed not to punish but to rehabilitate.

Or in the realm of personal tragedy, if we believe that this life is the only life, and death is the gate to nowhere, then we must fear it and mourn it without consolation. But if we believe that there is something imperishable within us, that death is not an end but a new beginning, then we have a philosophy about death that gives us courage to face it, and consolation when it takes our dear ones.

Is it important what a man believes? It is vitally important. It is important because by his beliefs man solves the problems of ethical choice from day to day.

But above all, it seems to me, what a man believes shapes his character. We become what we dream and what we hope.

Most of us recall Hawthorne's story, "The Great Stone Face." Above a little New England valley, a face was etched on the stone of the mountainside by wind and rain. It was a face full of calm repose, deep contentment, and spiritual uplift. It was believed that some day there would be someone in that valley whose face would resemble that of the great stone face. And Ernest, who was a little boy when the story opened, watched as the returning heroes, who had gone out from that valley to become warriors, thinkers, statesmen, returned, and people would compare them to the stone face. The poet came back, and his face had the sweetness but not the strength; the general returned—his face had the strength but not the gentleness of the great stone face. But daily Ernest worked, and daily he looked toward the mountainside. And then, when he was old and silver-gray, suddenly people began to see in Ernest the humble workman and quiet citizen, the same qualities that were possessed of the great stone face. Ernest had become the product of his dreams and aspirations.

It is a beautiful story, and I have told it often. But one day I was startled, and suddenly asked myself, "But what if the stone face had been cruel and malignant? What then would Ernest have become?"

It is not enough, you see, just to have beliefs. What a man believes is important because it shapes his character, and what he believes should be important to him, lest he shape the wrong character.

Faith and love need not be blind

In seeking the axioms upon which to build a theory of life and a structure of character, man needs to seek for the highest ideals, needs to go as far as the human mind can go to the very heart of things.

And the mind is important in this quest. To hear some people talk, you would think that faith, like love, must be blind. Some contemporary theologians talk of the failure of reason and the need for a "leap of faith" like a child who closes his eyes and holds his nose as he jumps off a diving board. And some opponents of religion say today, as they have said many times, that religion is irrational, that the spiritual truths cannot be proved, and therefore that religion is a form of ignorance or superstition.

It would be unfortunate to take such descriptions of faith, whether by its friends or its enemies, as the ultimate truth. To assume that faith and reason are mutually exclusive, that if you are intelligent you will not have faith, and if you are faithful, you cannot use your intelligence, would be a mistake.

A professor of mine used to solve this apparent problem in this fashion: Faith and Reason are like the two eyes in our head. *It takes both of them to see clearly and accurately.*

With one eye (try covering one of them) we can see shape and color, but we cannot determine depth or distance. With one eye we see only flatly. It takes two eyes to see depth. So it is with the eyes of reason and faith. With reason, we can see only the surface; faith gives us perspective, a sense of depth and insight which adds dimensions to life.

It is rather like love. Love is not blind, love sees more clearly. When we love someone, we see not only a face and figure, we see a character, a personality, a soul.

With reason, we see the universe, its structure, its order. With faith, we sense the Reason, the Intelligence, the Personality behind that universe, which gives it meaning and direction and purpose. Reason and faith are NOT mutually exclusive. They are like the two eyes in our head. We need them both.

With both mind and heart, man ought to seek the eternal values, and make them the axioms in the book of his life, that they may become the foundation of his ethics, the compass in his moral bewilderment, and the model for his development. What we believe we become.

2

Where Faith Begins

"This new revival of interest in religion is all the bunk," said the Cynic.

"Why?" I asked.

"Because it is based on fear," he replied.

"And what is wrong with that?"

"Religion ought to grow out of love," he said. "A faith that is born of desperation and nurtured on anxiety is no good."

"Just a minute," said I. "There is nothing wrong with a religion that grows out of fear, as long as it grows. Children come to love their parents out of helplessness. A baby is afraid, afraid of the dark, of loud noises, of being dropped. He first turns to his parents because they help him feel safe and secure. But his love does not stay on that level, at least not in happy families. As a child grows, he learns to love his parents not only for what they do for him, but for *what they are*. A child's fear grows into friendship. Is that love unworthy because it began in terror? In the same way, if a faith which begins in a foxhole grows into a companionship with God, does that make it bad?"

"Bosh!" said the Cynic. "Some sons do not write their fathers except when they need money."

"But I wasn't speaking of them," I concluded, "or of men who pray ONLY when they are in trouble. I am speaking of the boy who writes his dad just to say hello, and the man who prays to God when he is happy as well as when he is sad.

I do not care where a faith begins, if it just grows into a friendship with our Father in Heaven."

We don't know why

Such faith is not easily won nor easily held. There are unanswered questions which perplex the mind; there are emotional blocks which disturb the heart, and deep doubts that prevent assent.

These road blocks in the path toward faith need our thoughtful examination.

The unanswered questions of religion are most often asked by youngsters. My children ask me all sorts of questions I am hard put to answer. They want to know what God looks like. They ask me how He can hear so many bedtime prayers at once. They wonder why God made such awful things as mosquitoes and octopuses. They want to know why God let that little girl down the street die.

What shall we answer them? We can explain to them that God is not someone you can see, that He is not body but spirit. We can tell them in all sincerity that we believe that God does hear prayer, all prayers, that not a child whimpers in the darkness but that God is concerned. And when they puzzle over these answers, we tell them that they are still young, that when they are older they will understand these things. But sometimes we have to admit to our children, as we admit to ourselves, that we do *not* know the answers to some of their questions. We do pray, we believe that God hears prayer, but we do not know how. We lose a dear one by some terrible accident or dread disease, and we say: God has given, God has taken away. But we do not know why. We read about cities swallowed up by earthquakes, babies smothered in their own blankets, and we are like children ourselves. Why, we ask, why? And no answer is given.

Are these unanswered questions a threat to our faith? Does the fact that we cannot say why some things take place make our religion a matter of make-believe? Sometimes our young people tell us so. Sometimes a youth, with one or two years of college under his belt, will insist that our inability to answer these questions proves the falsehood of our faith, proves that the agnostic or the atheist has the better of the argument.

Is it so? I wonder.

I wonder if we have to know, to be able to prove, all religious truths or to answer all religious questions to justify our faith. Perhaps we can learn by parable.

Turn on the light of the spirit

A little child learns how to turn on the light in his room. He learns by experience that if he reaches up to the switch and pushes it, his light will go on. Does that child understand why? Does he know that there are wires from the switch to the light fixture, that what happens when he pushes a button is that he makes a connection between two metal parts which permits a flow of electric current? He does not. Yet he can turn on the light.

Well, of course, we know what he does not know. We know about the wires, the connections, the flow of electricity. We not only know how to turn on the light, we know how to wire the house, how to put in the switches, how to read the meter, how to fix it if it goes wrong. But wait a minute. Do we know any more than a child about electricity itself? Does anyone know what electricity really is? No one, no one at all, and yet we harness it, we use it, we brighten our homes, preserve our food, warm our bodies, heal our diseases with electricity that we do not understand, but have learned to use.

There are things, likewise, about religion that we do not understand; there are things about God that we do not know; yet we can turn on the light of the spirit, we can distinguish between right and wrong, we can make connection with Him through prayer. Little as we know about the source of our light, we can turn on the light. And this is the important thing—not the whys which we do not know how to answer, but the hows to which we have found the answer. Religion is effective, it works, whether we understand it fully or not. It has made saints out of sinners, martyrs of the weak in flesh; it has been the source of mankind's ideals and hopes and dreams. It works.

And if we still have questions, well, we might tell ourselves what we tell our children—that when we grow older we shall understand these things. One of the lovely word-pictures of rabbinic tradition was a depiction of the afterlife as a schoolroom in which eager pupils would learn directly from God the reasons for His actions, the purpose of His ways. We do not know why today; we shall know why tomorrow. But between today and tomorrow, let us live by the light we have.

3

"Getting Religion"

But not only are there questions that perplex the mind, there are questions which trouble the heart. One of them has to do with how one "gets religion." I have spent a good deal of time on campuses during the past twenty years, and one of the most frequent questions I am asked is this one. Precisely because there has been a religious revival and a "hunger for the word of the Lord," young people who would like to feel something in their hearts will ask, "How do I get religion?"

Now the reason the question is put this way is that, it seems to me, most people conceive of religious experience as being something like a bolt of lightning, a sudden flash of inspiration, and quickly what was dark becomes light, what was doubtful becomes certain. One minute you do not have religion, and the next moment you do. That's why people speak of "getting religion."

And, of course, some people do "get religion." They listen to Billy Graham and suddenly they feel like new persons; they stand by a seashore, and suddenly feel as though God is calling them by name; they stand in a saloon with a glass of whisky in their hand, put it down, walk out, and never touch the stuff again. And because such experiences are so dramatic, because they are so overwhelming, the person who feels a need for religion in his life may feel cheated if this is not the way he gets it.

But this is not the only way of getting religion. I do not believe that everyone gets religion the same way. I do not believe that everyone has to have a soul-shattering experience, a sudden revelation, a flash of lightning. I believe that many people grow in religion—that for them the experience of God is not like a flash of lightning so much as like a sunrise.

And I would say to young people who may feel as though they have not really got religion unless they have a dramatic conversion experience, that you may have religion without realizing it, and certainly you can get religion without the sudden conversion.

Let me illustrate by the analogy of the love of a man and a woman. Some people "fall in love." They meet each other on Tuesday at eleven o'clock, and at eleven-fifteen they are hopelessly head over heels in love, and by Thursday of the next week he has bought her a ring, and they are planning their wedding. It happens that way—you have seen it yourself. But is this the only way to fall in love?

Other people have known each other almost as long as they can remember. A boy and a girl live next door to each other; they go to school together, to their first parties together, to college together. They do not fall in love, but grow in love, something like a flower that buds, and then blossoms. If you ask them, "When did you know you loved each other?" they really cannot tell you. There was no sudden experience, but like the tide coming in, love slowly flooded their hearts.

Similarly, falling in love with the universe, "getting" faith in God can be the same way. It can be a sudden experience, or it can be a gradual experience. It can be like a flash flood from a cloudburst, or it can be like a slow swelling of streams in a spring thaw. And both ways are genuine.

So when young people ask me how they can get religion, I respond with a question, "How does one fall in love?" One falls in love by seeking the company of girls (or of boys) until you meet one with whom you fall in love or grow to love. So with religion. Go to services of worship, read the Bible, look out at nature's beauties, help people in distress, do the things that add to faith, and perhaps you will find God and fall in love with His world.

The test of your faith

One more word needs to be added. Whether a person gets religion or grows in faith, the type of experience is less important than what it does to him and what kind of person it makes him. If a marriage breaks up, it does not matter how the couple fell in love. Real conversion, whether dramatically sudden or gradual, involves a turning of the heart toward new goals, involves a powering of the spirit by new insights. The test of a faith is a life. How do you get religion? Seek God, seek Him with all your heart until you find Him, and finding Him, find life in its finest sense.

And if that fails? If the intellectual doubts continue, and the emotional desert fails to flower, what then? Every once in a while I meet people who have either lost their faith or never developed one. But because they are unsatisfied with agnosticism or atheism, they challenge me to prove the truths of religion. They want to believe, even though they lack faith.

And so they ask how human beings can have faith in God when there is so much suffering and misery in the world. If God is a good God, why does He allow evil men to destroy life? If God is compassionate, how can He permit disease to waste or pain to rack the human body? When we see all about us selfishness and cruelty and inhumanity, how can we still believe there is a divine Being?

Now I have discovered that there is very little point in answering these questions with any of the traditional replies. If I say, as do some theologians, that evil is not really evil, but only appears as such to man's shortsighted gaze, they reply, "Perhaps so, but it hurts, and what you say doesn't make it quit hurting."

If I say, as did Job, that God's purposes are higher than man's understanding, that in the divine plan of life there is a reason for everything, they will answer, "But if I cannot understand the reason, I cannot be satisfied with the event."

If I say, as do many, that without suffering there is no joy, without darkness there is no light, the agnostic replies, "That's all well and good for you. You have the light. But what about me, or about him? Where is our joy, our light?"

And if I quote the Bible, they ask how do we know the Bible speaks the truth? Or if I point out that the injustices of this world will be righted in the next, they insist that I prove to them that there is an afterlife.

No, the traditional answers will not help those who have lost their faith, because every idea about God and every explanation of evil in this world relies upon the very faith they have lost. If people will not believe or cannot believe, there is no point in saying to them, "You must believe." What they want is a proof of God that can be followed step by step, faith that can be demonstrated as clearly as a scientific formula. And there is no such proof. If there were, then obviously no one would have any doubts, no one would question. If it were as easy to prove the truth about religion as it is to prove that two and two make four, then no one would lose his faith.

This is why I cannot answer the man who has lost his faith in God with the traditional answer. I cannot begin where I am in my faith; I must begin where he is in his loss of faith.

Hold hands in the dark

The light of faith has gone out of his life; he is in the dark, and all that I can say to him is what I once heard a man say, "Hold hands in the dark." If, as you believe, men are like children lost in a dark forest without a compass or a Guide, then seek the companionship and fellowship of unhappy humanity and hold hands in the dark.

If life has lost its meaning for you, if the Eternal Light no longer burns in the Temple of your Soul, if for you there is no God but only purposeless suffering and meaningless misery, hold hands in the dark. If you believe that all men are wandering in a godless universe, if you doubt the Bible and doubt the teaching and doubt the care of a loving God, then hold hands in the dark.

What else, really, is there to do? In the presence of tragedy, would you merely curse the God in whom you lost faith, or set about healing the hurt that life has wrought? If there is no God to comfort the grief-stricken, then who but you can comfort them? If the universe looks on impassively when men shed tears, who but you can dry them? If there is no Voice from beyond to speak courage to men's hearts, then you must give them courage. If the world is black with night, then hold hands in the dark.

And it may be that if those who have lost their faith so live, it may be that if they who cannot accept the truths of religion so act, in compassion and in fellowship, in the darkness of their souls there will gleam a light, and out of the love and pity of their hearts there will come a flame that will bring light back to their lives, and they will discover God again by experience.

Faith is not easily won nor easily held.

It means being willing to hold to beliefs that cannot yet be fully explained, to live by whatever truths have grown in the heart, and to walk through the valley of the shadow of suffering and of doubt holding hands in the dark until the light goes on again.

4

Be Partners with God

Sometimes a striking phrase will say more than a whole book of philosophy. Occasionally, the truth is caught up in one gleaming jewel of speech. Once I was sailing with some friends on a Minnesota lake, and one of them said, "Man raises and lowers the sails; God makes the wind to blow."

What a perfect description of man's partnership with God, and of God's partnership with man! Everything about us is God's handiwork. The "laws" of nature which our sciences search out and discover are God's laws. The universe is His creation. God makes the wind to blow.

But still, it is man who raises and lowers the sails. Man depends upon the wind, but not like a tumbleweed which just goes where the wind blows. Man may depend upon the winds, but he uses them. He may scud along before them, he may angle across them, he may even tack against them and sail upstream. God makes the wind to blow; man raises and lowers the sails.

In the world of nature, therefore, in the world of physics and chemistry, man is at the helm of life. He is given a universe in which to be co-creator with God. God has made the atom; man may use its power for destruction or for creation.

But there is another sense in which this picturesque description of life is true; it applies to the spiritual realm of man's life.

God makes the wind of His spirit to blow; man raises and lowers the sails of his soul.

There is a prevailing moral wind which God breathes across man's heart. It blows in the direction of warmer affections, of wider horizons of brotherhood, toward the harbor called peace. But it is for man to raise or lower the sails. He can drift with the tides of indolence, run before the storms of passion, or he can seek to bring his craft to the promised port. God gives us the dream, but only we can fulfill it.

And if we try, sometimes a hand greater than our own completes the work we set out to do.

One summer at the beautiful "Y of the Rockies" in Colorado, I signed up for a class in landscape painting. The instructor took us to a spot from which we could view a breath-taking landscape, then let us go to work. I struggled to reproduce that view, but the more I mixed and the more I brushed, the more unhappy I became. I felt completely inadequate. Then, making his rounds of the students, the instructor came to my canvas. He explained that distant hills are best done in a hazy violet, and then, to illustrate, he mixed a little paint, and with two quick strokes outlined the mountain peak. Suddenly, with just that touch of a master's hand, my poor effort came to life and really began to look like the far-off hills.

Isn't this the way God sometimes completes the work we try so hard to do? We make desperate attempts to bring our plans to fruition, and often feel as though we have failed, but then God seems to take a hand, and out of our poor efforts something emerges more wonderful than we ever dreamed of. By way of illustration, I recall hearing a student at a class reunion say to his professor: "Do you remember the day you advised me about my career? You changed my whole life!" The professor said later that he had no recollection of what he had said. "When students turned to me for advice, I always felt so inadequate," he said. Somehow, God must have guided his words that day.

For sometimes a Hand greater than our own completes the work we set out to do.

If a child asks you

"How do you explain to a child why he cannot see God?"

This is a question that troubles many parents and many teachers. How can we explain an abstract idea to youngsters whose minds run to the concrete? Well, here is the way Mrs. Bertram Klausner, a rabbi's wife from St. Louis, said she would teach a child to understand about God.

"I would take a cup of warm water and let the child taste it. Then I would take some sugar and put it in that water, and let him taste it again. Then I would say to him: 'You could not see the sugar in the water, could you? But you knew it was there. You knew it was there because you could taste it.

"'So it is with God. You cannot see Him, but you know He is there, because He gives life its sweetness.'"

I have never heard a simpler nor sweeter explanation of a very difficult subject. I have been teaching children now for twenty-five years, and have never made it so clear as Mrs. Klausner, writing in the magazine *American Judaism*, made it. "God is like sugar dissolved in water. You cannot see Him, but He is there."

Isn't that what we mean, too, when we speak of the soul of man, of the Godlike within us? How else could you describe the soul, and how better? You can't see the soul. A medical student once crowed to me in an atheistic mood: "What do you mean by soul? I have had a human body on the dissecting table. I have examined every part of it, taken apart every muscle, explored the interior of the heart and liver and lungs. I have followed the nerve cables up into the cranium and taken apart each fiber of the brain, and never did I see a soul."

And I am sure he didn't. For I have never seen a soul either, but I know I have one. And I know he had one, too, for I said to him: "All right, so you have no soul, but tell me this: Did you find in the body the ideals that are part of you? Did you find in the heart the desire to heal people, or did you find the muscle that squeezes the tear sacs when you see a hungry child, or did you find the brain cell that says: Thou shalt not murder? None of these can be touched, and yet we feel them; none of them can be seen, yet we see by them. Your whole life, young doctor, is built on an ideal you cannot see, touch, or dissect. It is built on faith that human beings are worth healing."

No, we cannot see God, we cannot see the soul, but we know they are there; they change the taste of our lives.

This is so of love as well. You cannot see it, but you know it is there. Love is not hugging and kissing. Lots of folks hug and kiss without a bit of love between them. Love is a feeling—a feeling that someone is more important to you than life itself. Can you find that feeling, can you dissect it? No, it's like sugar, it makes life sweet.

Life without God would be as flat as warm water—no taste at all. Can you imagine living a life purely animal, so that a flower becomes something to crop and chew, a sunset simply a warning to nest down? Can you imagine a family life without God? A purely biological family life like an animal's, in which once the young are able to fend for themselves, there is no such thing as the love of parents and children? Can you imagine a society in which the strong would destroy the weak, the clever defraud the simple, the cruel lord it over the kind?

You see, what makes humanity human is the sweetness of God dissolved into the protoplasm of man—it's the yearning for light, for beauty, for truth, for goodness. It's the groping for better ways of living, and higher ways of loving. It's the dream of Jacob at Beth El, and the stern demand of Moses in Egypt to let his people go. It's the vision of Isaiah, the prayer

of Solomon. It is all the urgency of the human heart seeking
always to lift itself upwards. This is the soul, this is the presence of God in the human heart; this is what we try to teach
our children to know and to understand, that just as sugar,
unseen, sweetens water, so God, unseen, sweetens and en-
nobles life.

There is another way to tell children about God's care and
that is to describe Him as a loving Father who guides us
along life's paths.

A little hand in yours

My children are getting older now. (Isn't everybody?) They
have much more self-reliance than once they had, and independence too. There was a time, for example, when they
were not allowed to cross the street, any street, by themselves. Then as they grew, they had permission to cross quiet
streets on their own, but on busy streets they were still expected to take our hand. Now they are old enough to handle
themselves pretty well, to watch the traffic lights, and to
walk the busy streets without worrying too much about
them.

And yet, I have observed an interesting thing. If we are
walking together downtown and come to a corner where the
traffic is unusually heavy, where the crowds are thick and
the autombiles quick, then without my suggesting it, my
children will reach up and take my hand. Self-reliant as they
have become, there are times when they still turn to their
father for reassurance.

Isn't this true of all of us? In the normal flow of the traffic
in quiet streets, we manage to walk our ways without much
concern. We are capable of taking care of ourselves, of handling our own problems, of meeting our own needs. And then
when the traffic of life becomes thick and threatening, we
suddenly find that we are not so secure, that we need help,
and we reach up our hand to our Father in Heaven for re-

assurance. And He takes our hand, as it were. "He bends down close to the suffering to hear their cry."

We might stop here, except for one additional implication. A child does not reach his hand up to just any grownup standing by him. He seeks his own father who has loved him and whom he has learned to love in return through the years. Similarly, if we are to seek God in heavy traffic, we should already have learned to love Him on quiet paths. Let us, therefore, walk with Him in all the highways and byways of life, in our homes and sanctuaries, so that in good times or bad, we may reach up our hand for guidance, and find Him there.

5

The Real Answer to Prayer

"Why should we pray? What good does it do?" asked a pupil of mine.

I might have replied, "Because we cannot help it," and stopped there. For it is true that man prays almost as the mouth waters with the smell of food, or as a sunflower turns toward the light.

But a question like this deserves a fuller answer. Why ought we to pray?

In the first place, prayer is a way of increasing our sensitivity to the spiritual aspects of life. From this point of view, it is very much like exercise. A man's muscles become responsive by training. A football player will play scrimmage day after day until he begins to be able to sense what the other side is going to do almost before they do it. Or, if you want to learn to appreciate art, you not only go to look at it but try your hand at producing some, painting a picture or molding a statue, and suddenly you become conscious of all that is involved in the play of form, light and shadow, color and depth. Or take a few piano lessons and then go to a concert to hear a great pianist. Suddenly you are far more conscious than ever before of the movement of the hands, and the interpretation of the music. Exercise of any sort enlarges the capacity to understand, to appreciate, to react.

The soul is stretched and enlarged by prayer just as the body is stretched and enlarged by physical exercise. "O Lord, open my eyes that I may see truth and beauty in all Thy world, and Thy spirit in all things."

In the second place, prayer is good because it helps us conquer and control our appetites.

Someone has very aptly compared the human body to a wild horse. A wild horse is strong, spirited, speedy, and enduring, but also useless and even dangerous. But train that wild horse, break him in, gentle him, teach him to respond to orders, and he can become a magnificent and useful creature. So with the body and its appetites. Give it free rein, let it run wild, and it will kick and bite and run riot through life. But train that body, curb it, break it in, gentle it, and it becomes a tool of the personality, controlled power for great living. On a wild horse, you do not go where you want to go, but where the horse wants to go. With an uncontrolled body, you can only follow its appetites and whims, but under control it will take you where you wish to go. Prayer is a way of saying, "Whoa, boy" to the body; it is a way of putting a bridle and reins upon the passions. Prayer asks God to purify our hearts and to help us conquer our weakness.

And, finally, prayer is a way of aspiration. It is a way of lifting ourselves, of getting a higher look, of transcending self. For when a man looks at life only from inside himself, or only from within the walls of his home, or profession, seeing the world as though it were all in terms of *his* special interests, then he is "too full of himself to have any room for God." But in prayer, he sees life as God sees it, and relates his own little life and his own little needs to the needs and life of humanity. He lifts himself by prayer, and achieves a high spiritual stature.

Why pray? Pray to enlarge, to strengthen, and to lift the soul.

But there is a precondition for prayer, and that precondition is faith.

When prayer is in vain

In the widespread religious revival of our time, some curious things take place. One of them is what might be called play-acting at religion. I do not mean hypocrisy or pretending, but rather an attempt to induce religion by going through the motions.

A college student recently told me that his prayers were not producing any results. "Everybody talks about how prayer brings you peace of mind, a fresh outlook, solutions to life's problems," he said, "but when I pray, nothing happens."

"Do you believe in God?" I asked him.

"I'm not sure," he replied. "I would like to, but I do not really think I do."

"Then that is why your prayers are not satisfying you," I told him. "You are not really praying prayers, you are just going through the motions."

Professor Abraham Heschel, of the Jewish Theological Seminary in New York, has put it very neatly: "Prayer without faith is like a Hindu rope trick." The Hindu fakir produces a wonderful illusion: he throws a rope seemingly into the empty air and a boy climbs the rope! It cannot be done. You have to attach the rope to something before you can climb it. And so with prayer. You can toss it into the air, you can say, "The Lord is my Shepherd," but if you do not believe in the Lord, then you will still be in spiritual want.

Prayer is more than autosuggestion or self-hypnosis. Prayer is communication between man and God. If it is founded on a faith that just as man's body begins with materials outside him, so his yearnings, his restless longing for meaning, also begin outside him; that just as Nature is his mother, so God is his Father. Hunger is nature's way of keeping us alive, and the urge for prayer is God's way of keeping us spiritually alive. And when a man believes this, when he knows in his heart that prayer is more than words spoken into the air, that prayer can be communion with God, then it is that prayer begins to have meaning, and does create the inner mood which brings fresh moral challenge and deep peace of soul.

There is one warning note, however, which needs to be sounded, a warning against vain, useless, or irreverent prayer. The Talmud gives us an example. "If a man, coming home to his village, hears the sound of lamentation, and prays, 'May those who lament not be of my house,' this is a vain prayer."

Not that such a hope is unnatural. When we see smoke rising in the direction of our homes and hear the shriek of fire engines, the thought comes immediately to mind—oh I hope it's not our house.

But natural as it may be to think such a thought, it is wrong, according to the Talmud, to put that thought into prayer—it is a prayer in vain.

It is vain in the first place because it asks that what is already past be changed. This is a manifest absurdity. If the house has already caught fire, it is too late to pray that it not be on fire. If death has come to a home, it cannot be undone. It is too late; it is a vain prayer.

And it is vain in the second place because in a way it wishes the evil on others. When a man hears the sound of mourning, he knows that someone has passed away. For him, at that moment, to pray that it not be from his house is to pray that it be from someone else's house. In a way he is praying, "Let others mourn." Such a prayer is a selfish prayer.

Such prayers are vain in the third place because in a way they discredit all prayer. When prayer is reduced to selfish proportions, when it says to God, "Do *my* will, not Thine," then those whose religious ideas are not firm sense the vanity and narrowness of it and want nothing to do with it.

What, then, is the prayer a man should utter if he hears lamentation rising from his village? Let it be, "O Lord, if this mourning be in my home, give me courage to face what Thou hast willed."

Does God answer?

"How can I believe that God answers prayer?" asked my young friend. "There are billions of people in this world, millions of worlds in this universe. Why should God be concerned with my petty problems? How can I bother Him with my requests? And if I do, how can He drop everything He is doing to tend to my little needs?"

God *does* answer prayers; God *is* concerned with the life of every human being. And if you ask how can He who sets the stars in their courses and renews each day the work of creation, how can He have enough interest in or find enough time to be bothered with His human children, then listen to what Galileo once said.

"The sun is ninety-two million miles from the earth; it is the center of the solar system, and by the power of gravity holds every planet in its orbit. Yet that very same sun can ripen a bunch of grapes *as though that were all it had to do.*"

In similar fashion, the great God who created a universe larger than the mind of man can grasp still leans down to give men strength to meet their problems, to heal them in their diseases, to comfort them in their grief, as though that were all He had to do.

What shall we pray for?

Unfortunately, a popular idea of prayer is that it is a way of flattering and nagging God to get our way. When a little boy was asked one Saturday night why he had not said his usual prayers, he answered, "Oh, I don't want anything from God tonight." But when a child grows up, he realizes, or he should realize, that prayer is not trying to get God to change His mind about us, but getting us to change our minds about God; not an effort to persuade God to do *our* will, but an effort to lift us to the point where we will do God's will.

Prayer is not a push button to summon a heavenly bellhop. Prayer is a way of lifting us to a level where we know what to pray for; prayer is a way of defying fate and conquering misery; prayer is a way of releasing divine energy within us that we may, with God's help, answer the very prayers that we offer.

What shall we pray for? For bicycles, convertibles, dividends? We have not been taught so to pray. Our prayer book teaches us to ask for forgiveness or knowledge of God's law, for purity of heart, for those qualities and those spiritual insights which enable us to see God's will clearly and to pray as did Eliezer ben Hyrcanos, Talmudic sage, hundreds of years ago: "Do THY will in Heaven and give composure of spirit to those who worship Thee on earth." Prayer's purpose is not to change nature but human nature; not to ask God to break His laws, but to help us keep His laws.

I do not know whether prayer will bring rain to a drought-stricken Texas. But I do know that prayer will bring rain into a dried-up heart, warmth into a cold soul, calm into a stormy spirit. We come to God as a child does to his parents to pour out our troubles and find in His presence the courage to carry on. I have had the experience, you have too, of coming into a house of worship with all the ache and weariness of heart that we can bear—and then, in God's presence, leafing through the pages of the prayer book, hearing the music of religious yearning, and feeling the ache and the weariness and the pain fade away and new courage and new hope come to replace them.

Not long ago, a businessman came into our sanctuary, he told me, on a weekday, discouraged and hopeless. He had gone into business with too little capital, and now it looked as though he were about to go under. His business worries had, of course, reflected themselves in his personal health.

"I sat there for two hours," he said. "First I read some of my favorite prayers. Then I thought back over the events that led up to that day, what I had done or failed to do. And then I said, 'God, I've done everything I can do. From now on, it's up to You.' And would you believe it, Rabbi, that very week I got a couple of orders that kept me from closing and since then everything has been better."

Now I am not naïve enough to believe that God stood on the sidewalk outside that man's store and sent him some customers; but I am not sophisticated enough to believe that his prayers were of no avail. It seems to me that the very calm and quiet resignation which came to him in the sanctuary produced those changes in personality which had their subsequent effect.

It is this which is the *real* answer to prayer, when God says YES to our pleas for strength, courage, hope, insight. God does answer prayer. He does not fight our battles for us, but He gives us strength to fight them for ourselves. He does not conquer proverty for us, but He gives us the insight to conquer it for ourselves.

Sincere prayer can heal

PRAYER ALSO HELPS TO HEAL OUR DISEASES. We in religion have known this intuitively for a long time; today doctors are discovering it scientifically.

We are not a package containing three separate identities: a body, a mind, and a soul. We are one, and what happens to one part of us inevitably affects all of us. Sometimes physical pain is local, our foot hurts or our tooth aches, but sometimes physical difficulties in our stomach will give us a headache, and flat feet may make our back ache. The same thing is true from mind or heart to body. The improper functioning of our minds or of our personalities can make our bodies sick. We can make ourselves ill and we do make ourselves ill. We fret and worry and have anxieties, and the result may be ulcers or heart tremors. We boil with anger or burn with resentment and the heat affects our bodies. We go through an emotional storm, and a sinus attack is the result. Our emotions and our thinking do cause us to have pains and to feel sick.

The exploration of this area of life has become a full-fledged science of psychosomatics, research into the interplay between body and mind, between our souls and our organs.

Men who are studying the sick from the point of view of the whole personality are discovering that disease is caused not only by physical viruses and germs but by the psychological virus of resentment and germs of hate; not only by vitamin deficiencies but by affection deficiencies; not only by infections but by neglect, by nagging, by a loss of self-confidence, or a lack of faith. In other words, if we begin with a sick heart, we end with a sick body.

This is also true in reverse. If our bodies are sick, they can be cured not only by medicines, drugs, operations, or transfusions; they can be cured by a healthy mental attitude and a strong emotional adustment. A radiant personality, a deep faith in God are just as important to the curing of disease as penicillin or streptomycin. It has been pretty well proved for all except the most skeptical that sincere prayer can lengthen life.

Faith is not the only element in healing, but it is an important, a vital, perhaps even the most important, element. The patient who lies in a hospital bed and worries about problems at home, or who is apprehensive about the future, or who rebels against God, retards his own recovery. But the patient who is cheerful, who does not sink into morose self-pity, who is optimistic about himself, his family, and the world, will speed his own recovery.

I have sat by the side of many a sickbed, and I have observed it as a regular thing—the man or woman who talks to God in prayer, and does that talking in complete faith that God hears prayer, almost invariably improves with rapidity, and even in hopeless cases, faces pain and death with considerably more courage.

And what I have observed has also been observed by the surgeon who said, "In operative cases, prayer reduces muscular tension, lowers blood pressure and helps produce a more favorable reaction to anesthesia." Heal me, O Lord, and I shall be healed, is a prayer that can be answered.

Our minds do affect the health of our bodies. The emotions of our hearts do make a difference in our energies. The depth of our faith does have results in the field of medicine.

For radiant health, then, we need not only a balanced diet but a balanced personality, not only clean bodies but pure hearts, not only exercise of the muscles but exercise of religion, not only rest and relaxation but a sense of security in God's arms. We need to turn our hearts outward rather than inward, to release the tensions that build up inside us. We need to get insight into why we worry and why we feel resentment. We need to attain peace of mind before we can maintain a healthy body. It may sound flippant, but the road back to health is by a pill and a prayer. The secret of health is an active faith in God.

Three ways to be sure

MAN PRAYS TO GOD; GOD SPEAKS TO MAN.

A child in our religious school once asked me: "Rabbi, how do people know when God is speaking to them? I never heard Him say anything to me. Do you think I ever will?"

The first reply I gave that child was the same that you would give: God speaks to us through our conscience. When we are tempted to do something wrong, and a little voice says, "No, Jeannie, no," or when we see some little child being bullied, or a helpless puppy with a tin can tied to its tail and we hear a voice inside urging us, "Help, Jeannie, help him," that is God speaking to us. God's voice is a still small voice of conscience.

"But that's my voice," said Jeannie. "I want to know how God speaks." And this, of course, is a vital question. How does God speak? How did He speak to Moses, to Amos, to Malachi?

I think we might answer this question out of our own experience. All of us have had occasional moments of wordless wonder, when something aroused in us a sudden sense of beauty so great, or goodness so large, that we stood in speechless awe. It is then that our hearts were hushed and still, and in that quietness, although we heard no sound, no voice, no words, we still heard God.

And what is it that He says? He says whatever we now say that is different from before; after such inspired moments, we no longer think as we did, nor speak as we did. We have new thoughts to communicate, new ideas to put forth, and those new ideas are God's words. Out of the wordless deeps of communion there come words through our hearts and out of our mouths.

Surely this must have been what the prophets meant when they said, "Hear the word of the Lord!" Of course, they were geniuses of religion; theirs was a deeper experience than ours, their silences issued in greater language. But the very fact that we recognize their words as God's words points to the fact that He speaks to us as He spoke to them, in the inspired stillness of the soul.

I told this to a college student who asked the same question that Jeannie had, but he was not quite satisfied. "How can I be sure," he asked, "that what I say after such an experience is really and truly God speaking through me?"

There are three ways to tell whether the voice you heard is the voice of God. In a way, all three of them are negative tests, but they all have their positive side.

The first way to know if it is God's voice is whether it says to you, "Watch out for number one." If the voice you hear speaks of your getting ahead in the world, if it suggests that you will get a good reputation, if it says be careful not to get caught, that is not the voice of God. You will not hear the voice of God giving you practical advice on success, on how to make a million, on how to be a better salesman, on how to achieve your ambitions. These voices may be good voices, earnest voices, but they will not be the voice of God. God is not concerned with physical success; He is concerned with moral and spiritual success; He is not concerned in your making a million, but in your living for millions. The voice of God will not be the voice that says, "Watch out for number one." The voice of God will say, "Forget yourself, forget *your* needs, *your* desires, *your* ambitions." This is the first test by which to know if it is God's voice you hear.

The second test is, Does that voice tell you to be careful? Does it say, "Don't try to be a hero, don't be a martyr, don't stick your neck out"? If it does, it is not the voice of God. God is not concerned with our physical safety; God is not interested in our comfort, our ease, our lack of involvement in the lives of those around us. God never tells man to turn his back on life or life's problems, to turn his back on society and society's problems. God's voice never says, "Be careful." If anything, God's voice says, "Be uncomfortable."

Do you question this? Then read the Bible. God gave Abraham an unsettling order: "Get thee out of thy native land and away from thy father's house." God did not say to Moses: "Those slaves are none of your business, you just settle down here in Midian and enjoy life." He said: "Go down to Egypt." Jeremiah complained about God's voice—it brought him only trouble: the derision and the enmity of the rulers. "Yet the word of the Lord was like a raging fire within me and I could not keep silent." God's voice never says, "Be comfortable." God's voice always demands the uncomfortable, the sacrificial, the heroic. Religion does offer man peace of mind, but that does not mean peace of body. Peace of mind is not the result of comfort, but from being sure in faith.

The third test of God's voice is equally important. Does it tell you to hate? Does it arouse a fanatic fire that would sweep through the world in destruction? If so, it is not God's voice. God's voice will always say, "Thou shalt love thy neighbor as thyself." And if it says otherwise, beware! There is a perceptive illustration of this in an ancient Talmudic story. Rabbi Meir was annoyed by a group of godless men in his neighborhood. One day, in an excess of anger and exasperation, he stamped his feet and shouted, "May God destroy those evil men!" His wife, the gentle Beruriah, said, "Shush, Meir, you blaspheme. God does not 'desire the death of the sinner but that he return from his ways and live.' Therefore, let your prayer be: 'May God destroy the evil, but not the evil doers.'" It is good to hate evil, to uproot corruption and wrongdoing. Man must do all that he can to eliminate the wrongs of life, but his hatred must be for conditions and not people. The voice of God is a voice of love.

Man's conscience, you see, is a medley of voices. In his inner mind there are the sounds of many—the lessons his parents taught him, the voice of society, the lurking offstage cues of selfishness and of hatred, but the voice that is or should be above them all is the voice that speaks of spiritual, not material, success, that, while speaking of peace of mind, demands heroism of the body, that speaks of love for mankind. This, I believe, is the way to recognize the voice of God.

6

Your Moral Freedom

Man's moral freedom is emphasized and re-emphasized by
Jewish tradition.

The Talmud expressed it in a lovely legend.

"When a woman conceives a baby, an angel carries the
unborn soul before God and God decrees the fate of that
soul, whether it will be male or female, strong or weak, tall
or short, beautiful or plain, healthy or sickly, fat or thin.
Then the angel takes the soul for a tour of Paradise and
Gehenna, pointing out the rewards and the punishments that
are reserved for mortals when their lives are ended.

"Then the angel flips the baby on the upper lip so that he
forgets all that he has seen (hence the little hollow in our
upper lip) and he comes into the world crying because he
has lost a place of shelter, security and rest."

There are so many "modern" truths in this ancient legend.
Some schools of psychiatry have made much of the trauma
of birth and of man's desires for the security he once knew in
the womb. It is also true that through God's laws of nature
our chromosomatic fate *is* determined at the moment of con-
ception—whether we shall be male or female, of strong constitution or weak, beautiful or plain, tall or short.

But alongside these physical and psychological truths,
there is an all-important spiritual truth. Nowhere in the legend are we told that God foretells the unborn soul's character. Fat or thin is predicted, healthy or sickly too, but never

good or bad. This is left to the determination of man. This is left to the moral freedom of a human being.

Our moral fate, our evil or our goodness, our selfishness or our altruism, our hatreds or our loves—these are left altogether to the free will of human beings. No one can excuse the evil he does as the result of his fate; no one can take man's freedom from him.

Our moral freedom is a challenge.

It is also a source of unhappiness and misery. Anyone sensitive to life's tragedies will ask, sooner or later, how God can permit evildoers to run rampant through life; how He can allow villains like Hitler to destroy millions of men. Why does not God, if He be good, prevent man's cruelty to man?

No answer has ever been more clear-cut or plainly spoken than that of Rabbi Akiba, some eighteen hundred years ago. "Everything," said Rabbi Akiba, "is in the power of Heaven, except reverence for Heaven." God is all-powerful; He can do anything, anything except control the will of a human being. He cannot force men to love Him; He cannot force men to obey Him. He may be able to punish man, but He cannot prevent his doing what He punishes him for.

Akiba underlines the doctrine that man is free to choose good or evil. And man can misuse his freedom. God does not send a drunken driver to smash our bodies. God does not send a war to destroy our cities. These things we bring upon ourselves; they are the consequence of *our* choices, and *our* failures. And while it is true that the innocent are caught up in the evil done by the guilty, it is also true that all of us are responsible for the actions of our fellow men as well as our own. God has given us our freedom to choose good or evil. He cannot force our choice of good or prevent our selection of evil. "Everything is in the power of Heaven except reverence for Heaven."

But this does not imply that God is indifferent to our choices. He has not put us in "business for ourselves" and left us to run it as best we may. While He cannot prevent our evil, He stands ever ready to help us when we do good.

This idea is put in a very homely parable quoted in Benjamin Siegel's *The Sword and the Promise:* "God is like unto a storekeeper. If, in a store, one seeks to purchase pitch and sulphur, the storekeeper merely nods in its direction and says, 'Wait on yourself.' But if a customer wants to buy a pair of wings or try out a harp, the storekeeper is pleased to wait on him."

So with the Almighty. If we seek the paths of selfishness, of viciousness, God lets us wait on ourselves, but if we choose to do good, God helps us. And many a person can testify to this truth. Seeking light, they feel as though someone had turned on the switch. Failing in power, they had found new strength. Despairing in heart, they have been lifted by hope.

Nations, too, are governed by this law. How else can we explain the fall of mighty empires? How else understand the victory of the few over the many, the weak over the strong?

When men and nations shop for pitch and sulphur, God sends them to the self-service department. But when, on the other hand, they try on wings, God Himself waits on them and helps them.

The law of retribution

Not only does the universe encourage righteousness, it also discourages the choice of evil.

The moral law of retribution lies deep in the nature of things and is as sure as the laws of physics. Our failure to realize this is responsible for much of our unhappiness, both our personal tragedies and our social disasters.

This moral law can be illustrated by an analogy to the law of gravity.

According to the law of gravity, any two objects, regardless of size and weight, will, all things being equal, fall to the ground with equal speed. This law would seem untrue to our experience. Drop a feather from one hand and a bullet from the other, and the bullet will reach the ground first. But this does not disprove the law, for in this situation all things are not equal. Put both the feather and the bullet in a vacuum so that the feather has no air to float on, and they *will* drop at the same speed.

So it is with the moral law of retribution.

But the reason we do not see this clearly is that we drop moral bullets and moral feathers in the open air. And they do not fall at the same speed. The moral law likewise should have its qualifying phrase: all things being equal. But the difficulty is that there is no vacuum in life by which to experiment; we cannot make all things equal in human existence so as to test the validity of the moral law.

Must we then take it on faith alone? Is all that we can say that it is true whether you see it or not? Or is there a way of testing the moral law in a way which might prove it?

There is a way. It is the way of history. History is the test tube of the moral laboratory. In one lifetime, the moral law may seem not to work, but in the life of mankind, it has proved itself as certain as the law of gravity.

It is a moral law, for example, as fixed as the stars in their courses, that tyranny cannot long endure, that tyrants will inevitably come to naught. The tyranny of Egyptian Pharaohs, of Babylonian monarchs, of Assyrian conquerors, of Roman Caesars, lasted a generation, a century, sometimes even a millenium, but all of them, without exception, fell. And will always fall! We have seen it in our own time. Surely the suicide of Hitler in a Berlin bunker or the sight of Mussolini hanging by his feet while his people spat in his dead face ought to convince us. And while Stalin died in his bed, he was not allowed to rest in peace for long.

The names of those who once scourged the earth, whose power seemed to extend over the known world, are forgotten, while the memory of men like Moses and Jeremiah are fresh and green. The moral law is a sure law. It works as inevitably as the law of gravity.

To take another example, our religion teaches us the moral law that the welfare of human beings is inextricably intertwined, that we are our brothers' keeper.

Is this merely a pious wish or an unbreakable law? Look to the laboratory of life, look to history. Whenever men have looked on unmoved while their fellow men have suffered, whenever men have turned their backs on the tears of their fellow men, they have ended by being caught up in the same web of misery. Let an epidemic break out in the slums because those who live in nicer sections do not care and make no provision, and it will move into their homes. When a Mussolini attacks Ethiopia, when a Japan attacks Manchuria, and we say, "It's none of our business," then we end by putting on *our* uniforms and going off to war. Every man's fate is bound up with his brothers'. This is a moral law as unbreakable as the law of gravity.

Our moral freedom challenges us to shape the clay of our own lives, and to do what we can to mold the life of mankind.

Fatalism is fatal

Not everyone agrees to this thesis. There are philosophical and popular conceptions that deny man's freedom, that make him the puppet of fate. These range from Kismet to astrology, from assorted superstitions to systematic fatalism.

Every once in a while I am engaged in animated debate by a fatalist, by someone who believes that all of human life is controlled by forces outside the human being's own will power. Everything that is, had to be, and everything that will be, will be. Our lives are rather like listening to daily broadcasts of a soap opera. We may not know what the next episode will bring, but the author does.

Such theories of fate meet some deep needs.

First of all, we want to know the future. Striking blindly

out into tomorrow, we worry about the outcome of our enterprises. And so we consult the oracles, the seers, the soothsayers, the diviners and palm readers in the hope that somehow we can rend the veil of time and peer into the unknown tomorrow.

Secondly, we want to understand the accidents of life. Why does one man strike oil and another not? Why is one person sick and another healthy? One dies before his time, and another lives to a ripe old age. Fate, luck, becomes an answer.

And thirdly, we want to evade responsibility for our mistakes. If life is governed by four-leaf clovers and broken mirrors, or if our temperament is determined by the bumps on our head, or the star under which we were born, then we cannot be held responsible for our nature and the acts that flow from that nature.

Such are the needs which fatalism satisfies.

But there are also some other consequences which must be understood. Fatalism is fatal to man's and mankind's growth, because it nullifies our responsibility and paralyzes our will. If we are like flies in some web, then what's the point of worry and of struggle? If it is fated that the fly escape, he will escape, and if not, then struggle as he may, the spider will have his predestined lunch. As for the passer-by, why should he turn aside to release the fly? What is to be, will be; if the fly's number has come up, what difference whether he dies by the spider or by some other agent?

Actually, I have never met so complete a fatalist. Even those who argue for it theoretically do not tempt it in actuality. They, too, are careful of the way they cross the street; they, too, go to a doctor when they feel ill; they, too, try to take their fate into their own hands, and do what seems prudent and sensible.

Nathan Even-this

There is a Talmudic character whose ideas are pertinent to this subject. He had an unusual name, Nathan Even-this. Actually, his name was Ebenthiz, but they called him Even-this because he had a habit of saying, no matter what happened, "Even this is for the best." Let tragedy or sorrow befall him, he would say with quiet assurance, "Even this is for the best."

I have heard people echo this profound thought in a very shallow way.

A salesman regarded it as a great misfortune when the hotel he wished to stay in was out of rooms and had to send him to another hostelry. But when a fire razed the building he had been denied, he echoed Nathan Even-this. The morgue was full of charred bodies, but *he* was safe. To react in such a way, to say that everything is for the best as long as I escape the worst, is a bland and blind self-centeredness.

What Nathan Even-this really meant, I believe, was this: Even this CAN be for good. It does not say with a sort of vacuous optimism that everything inevitably results in good; it says with far more realism that the evil which does befall human beings can be turned into good, can be transformed into blessing.

Who of us cannot testify to this truth? All of us can look back at occasions which at the time seemed a terrible blow to our hopes—the loss of a job, a broken engagement, a business failure, but in the perspective of time we see that the very experience which seemed the worst awakened us and forced us to re-think our life, reshape our personality.

A famous golf champion used to say that he never learned anything from a victory, only from defeat, because when he lost a tournament he would go to a golf teacher and say, "Tell me what I am doing wrong."

Let us, then, understand the deepest meaning of Nathan Even-this's teaching. Things are not for the best because they happen to turn out well for me no matter what happens to others. Things are for the best only if intelligent and prayerful minds and hearts make them for the best, only if men with faith in God will struggle to turn every disaster and defeat into blessing.

This whole matter of freedom and fatalism is summed up in a Day of Atonement prayer.

That prayer begins with a picture of God writing in the book of life each man's fate for the year to come in words that are unmistakable: "Who shall live and who shall die; who shall succeed and who shall fail; who be well and who sick; who be rich and who poor."

It reminds us of Omar Khayyám's "the moving finger writes," but the prayer does not continue with Khayyám's "and having writ moves on, nor all your piety nor wit shall lure it back to cancel half a line, nor all your tears wash out a word of it. . . ." On the contrary, the Atonement prayer offers hope: "BUT repentance, prayer and deeds of loving-kindness will change the evil decree." Man's fate is decreed by God. Retribution for evil is a moral law. But man, in his moral freedom, can change his fate and suspend his sentence.

We are morally free. We have not chosen the parents to whom we were born, nor the age in which we live. But we have a choice as to whether to honor or dishonor those parents, whether to take part in solving that age's problems. No theory of fatalism can take that freedom of choice away. "Behold, I have set before you good and evil, life and death. Now choose good that you may live."

7

Make Love Your Goal

I don't need your synagogue and your prayer book," said my cynical friend. "*My religion is doing good.* I don't like these hypocrites who pray to God, and then prey on their fellow men, or the nicely pious who talk such a goody-goody religion but still hate everybody. So don't ask me to join, and don't ask me to come. My religion is doing good."

"Mine is too, my cynical friend," I replied. "If religion does not issue in doing good, then it is hypocritical and a pious fraud. Religion without ethics is no religion; but ethics without religion cannot stand for long.

"You say your religion is doing good. Without religion, how do you know what good is? Without religion, without faith in God, what makes one way better than another? Why is peace better than war, or co-operation better than quarreling, or charity better than cruelty? No, doing good is not a religion; doing good is the result of a religion. And what you are doing is living on the religion of others. You are taking what religion teaches is good and doing it, without supporting the institutions which keep alive the very idea.

"Look, friend, would you neglect the apple tree because all you believe in is eating apples, and you do not think leaves and bark are important? Religion and ethics are like a tree and its fruit. Cut down the tree or let it wither from lack of nourishment, and you won't have fruit for long.

"You say there are hypocrites in the pews. Of course there

are. But because one apple has a worm in it does not make the whole tree worthless.

"No, once you let the institutions of religion die or waste away you open the door to a religion of doing not good but bad. Look at Nazi Germany. Look at Soviet Russia. In both countries the synagogue doors were closed, the churches were put off limits, religion was labeled an enemy of the state, and the state became an enemy of religion. And what happened? Did ethics survive? Did the religion of doing good manage to live? On the contrary, when the tree was felled it no longer gave fruit, and barbarism replaced civilization.

"If your religion is doing good, go on and do good, but do not forget the tree on which your ethical fruit grew."

Both faith and works are important. Some say men are saved by faith, others say men are saved by works. But actually faith and works are two sides of the same coin. Faith is internal, deeds are external. One mirrors the other.

If you see a man whose hands drip with the blood of his neighbor, and whose mouth is foul with false witness, what kind of heart do you think he has? And if he boasts of having been saved, you can reasonably reply, "If you were really saved, you would not act thus; your actions speak louder than your words."

And on the other hand, if you saw a person who was kindly and sweet, helpful and self-sacrificing, you would assume without hesitation that a fine religious faith animated those acts.

The Talmud puts the same idea in very pithy language. "If a man steals wheat, grinds it to flour and from it makes himself a loaf of bread, and then, before eating it, says a prayer over food, that man does not pray, he blasphemes."

Faith and works are not mutually exclusive; faith leads to works and works test faith.

There is the same relationship between the spirit and the law, between the heart's desire and the hand's action, between the law of love and the laws of ethics. The love of one's fellow man, summarized in the Golden Rule, is too often contrasted with "legalism," with jots and tittles, when actually they, too, are in organic relationship. Both are necessary to guide man to the good life.

A law and the law

This was brought out by Hillel, a rabbi of the first century B.C.E., whom a pagan challenged: "I want your faith in a capsule. Tell me everything that Judaism teaches in the time I can balance myself on one foot."

Hillel's answer was a masterpiece. "What is hateful to thee, do not unto others. This is the law, all the rest is commentary. Now go and study the commentary."

Love is the overriding principle; the laws are the detailed expression of that love. For example, good driving is based on consideration, on love of neighbor. It is achieved by obeying the traffic signals. So, too, the Bible enunciates the great commandment of neighborly love, then continues with the moral traffic lights of daily human conduct.

The same idea is reinforced by a verse from the Book of Proverbs: "For the commandment is a lamp and the law is a light."

To the rabbis of old, this was more than poetic parallelism which said the same thing twice but in different words. This verse was comparing and contrasting the individual commandment and the total law. "The commandment is a lamp." This meant that when a man fulfills a commandment, he is like someone who carries a lamp into a dark room. "The law is a light" means something different. No matter how many candles are lit from a flame, the flame is not diminished. The law is like the pilot light on a stove; it never goes out. The verse, therefore, says that the commandment is a lamp kindled from the light of the law.

This rabbinic interpretation helps us recognize the distinction between *a* law and *the* law, between principle and application, between religion and morality. Religion is the flame on the altar, morality is the lamp which is lit at that flame.

From this point of view the Bible becomes the pilot light of our lives. We may no longer live by its every commandment, but we warm our lives by the spirit of its law.

So likewise is religion the pilot light of our democracy. From it we have learned the self-evident truths about God and man. From that pilot light of faith, we kindle the lamps of democracy which protect and enhance the dignity and the brotherhood of man.

There is still another way to relate the law of love and the detailed laws of morality.

"Thou shalt love thy neighbor as thyself" is so often spoken of as the first commandment; but it could also be thought of as the last. Love for our fellow men, absolute and constant and universal love for all men, is not the beginning of life but the *goal* of life.

It is rather like the four-minute mile for a runner. No young man begins by trying for a four-minute mile; he begins by training toward a four-minute mile. He learns to stride with the least effort, to control his breathing for maximum effectiveness, to measure his pace until the time comes for a sprint, and then, after months or even years of self-discipline, he begins to strike out for the four-minute mile.

So it is that God gives His children many commandments that lead up to the law of love. "Thou shalt" and "thou shalt not" are given in profusion. Even *before* we have learned to love all our neighbors as ourselves, we are bidden not to steal from them, not to strike them, not to covet what is theirs. Even before we have learned to love all our neighbors, we are urged to give charity to the widow, to protect the orphan, to show consideration to the maimed.

Now it is perfectly possible to perform all the commandments without any love, to behave somewhat like a sullen child who obeys his parents without giving himself or them any satisfaction. This may not be ideal, but it is better by far than disobedience. And the world in which no man would murder, nor steal, nor covet, nor bear false witness would not be too bad a world.

But, of course, love would make it even better. The law of love is like the top rung on a ladder by which man climbs, step by step, toward the Kingdom.

And above all, the good life is the product of a deep and abiding religious faith which expresses itself in moral self-direction.

We ain't livin' as good as we know how

Our age, however, has a naïve faith in education. One evening a group of us were discussing current problems. Juvenile delinquency came up. "We need to educate these youngsters," said one of the party.

Political corruption was brought into the picture. "The public needs to be educated," said another.

The decay in morality and family life was introduced. "Failure of education," was the comment of several.

And I could not help telling one of my favorite stories. A new county farm agent was full of ideas. He organized a course of lectures on improved agricultural methods and then set about recruiting a class. But he was stopped in his tracks when one old grizzled farmer replied to his proposals for education with devastating frankness, "Nope, sonny, no classes for me. I ain't farmin' as good as I know how now!"

All talk of more education and better education leaves me somewhat skeptical. Not that we should not do everything we can to provide religious and moral education for our youngsters, but we cannot put all our hopes in the teaching of these ethical truths.

Are we ignorant of what is right and wrong? Does the child, caught with his hand in the cookie jar, ever argue that he did not know it was wrong? Or does the politician, caught in the same embarrassing position?

Does the businessman, exposed for some tax evasion, ever

say, "I didn't know any better"? Or the labor leader who "borrowed" union funds?

It isn't moral knowledge that we need. "We ain't livin' as good as we know how now."

What we need is not more knowledge but more strength; not more ethical information but more moral fiber; not more teaching but more self-control. We need to begin living as well as we know how now.

No one is ignorant of the Ten Commandments; no one has failed to be taught the Golden Rule.

It is not in education, but in prayer, in self-discipline, in self-direction, that salvation lies in family life, in politics, in the whole world. We know enough now to live good lives, *if only we would.*

8

Reward and Punishment

I used to think it would be a wonderful thing if the wrongs men do could have a built-in punishment. It would be so simple to live a good life if every time we did something wrong, we would get slapped down immediately. Imagine something like a burglar alarm which would sound a gong each time we were tempted to step off the straight and narrow. Eddie Cantor used to say, "Oh, for a pastrami that would give you heartburn immediately instead of at two o'clock in the morning." But would it make any difference, really? Heavy drinkers know what a hangover is like, and as they down their sixth, you can hear them moaning, "Oh, what a head I'm going to have tomorrow."

I remember a man who served two years for forgery. He was released on Tuesday and came to Houston. On Wednesday he passed a bad check. In New York, you know, four convictions for crime means life imprisonment. You'd think a man would stop at four. But he doesn't.

It looks as though all of us are susceptible, that we do things we know will get us into trouble, and *we know it while we do it*. And if some inventor were to design a machine that would give us a shock every time we set out to do what we know will give us a bad time, many of us would probably try to figure out how to short-circuit the machine!

Why? Are we naturally perverse? I can hardly believe that. It would be an excuse, but not a reason. Do we think that perhaps just this one time we'll get away with it? We have learned better than that. The explanation is a simple one. Our emotions are strong, and our wills are weak. Ultimately, therefore, no punishment from the outside can help. Only a powerful determination on the inside can make any difference.

The Ethics of the Fathers stated this in one sentence: "Who is a mighty man? He who has conquered himself." The good life, the temperate life, the honest and considerate life requires daily heroism—the heroism of people who have restrained themselves. A runaway horse is easier to stop than a runaway emotion. People used to get medals for stopping runaway horses. They ought to be decorated for putting a checkrein on themselves.

And just as the controls are not external but internal, so are the rewards and punishments.

The only sure reward

The only sure reward on this earth for our good deeds is the spiritual satisfaction of having done them. Sometimes they may bring us material blessings, but just as often they do not; and to expect "payment" for our virtues is to fly in the face of experience and to rob ourselves of the joys of goodness.

There is a charming illustration of this idea in a little rabbinic tale. A man once came to his rabbi with this question: "Rabbi, when I was a boy, I read in *The Ethics of the Fathers:* 'He who seeks honor, honor flees from him, but he who runs from honor, honor will catch up with him.' Now, Rabbi, if this is so, tell me how it is that all my life I have been running from honors, and honor has not caught up with me."

The rabbi gave him a long, slow look, then said, "Perhaps it is because you have been looking over your shoulder."

We do look over our shoulders. We do the right thing, we try to live ethically and lovingly, but so often with a covert hope that our efforts will be applauded, that we shall gain friends, or influence, or honor. And when these fail to materialize, we become sour with disappointment and bitter with disillusionment.

We ought not to expect any rewards for our goodness. Not even the kind that come up from behind. "The reward of a good deed is a good deed," said the Talmud. This does not mean that if I scratch your back, you will scratch mine. No, it means that the return for an act of kindness is the strength and the opportunity for another act of kindness.

This is all the reward we can expect or demand; it is the only sure reward on this earth. But believe me, it is worth it.

The stuff of which Hell is made

On the other hand, the worst punishment a human being can suffer on this earth is to be caught in the act. The feeling of shame is pure agony.

Most of us can remember, for example, when our mother caught us in a lie. We can all recall how we felt as we stood there in front of her and she looked deep into our eyes and asked if we were really telling the truth. It was sheer misery to return her gaze; it would have been easier to take a "licking." We would rather have looked any place else in the world. We would have done anything in the world to erase the lie that was spoken. What a relief it always was to break down in tears, confess our lie, and be forgiven.

But what if there had been no chance to confess and be reconciled? Can you imagine what it would be like to carry a sense of shame for eternity?

This is what Esdras (in the Apocrypha) describes as the stuff of which Hell is made. When a wicked man dies, Esdras reports the angel as telling him his first stage of punishment is the realization that it is too late to repent, and the seventh and worst stage is to stand ashamed forever in the presence of God.

It seems to me that Esdras shows a real insight. No one knows what Heaven and Hell are really like, but if life makes sense, then surely they cannot be very different from this world. What finer Heaven could there be than one in which love continues? What worse Hell than the Hell of shame? Brimstone and hellfire would be easier to bear.

A sense of shame is one sort of Hell on earth. Another sort is recorded by Esther Salaman in her memoirs, *The Fertile Plain*.

"My mother once said: 'I've never seen a bad man go unpunished. Of course, our accounts and His don't always tally. He chooses His time and means. I used to ask God, when I would see E. (who had foreclosed on widows and robbed orphans) prosperous, in good health and with a large family, why it was like that. When your father died young and E. was still hale and hearty, I used to grumble to God. Then I heard something which stuck in my mind. Someone told me once, "Whenever I meet old E. he starts asking me about the S. family, and talks about their prosperity and about the house they own with bitter envy. Why? It isn't as if his own sons were unsuccessful and hadn't got houses of their own?" Then I knew. I'd expected God to punish him by making him poor or sick, but isn't it a greater punishment to be plagued with envy?' "

The Talmud reinforces this idea. One of its sages pondered the nature of Hell as described in various Biblical prophecies and finally concluded that Hell is neither a time nor a place.

The words, "Behold a day cometh, it burns as a furnace" suggests that Hell is a period of time.

And the words, "Whose fire is in Zion" suggests that Hell is in a particular place.

But the reality of Hell is described best, the Talmudic sage asserted, in the words, "Your breath is a fire that shall devour you." The wicked will die in their own flames. Men *are* consumed by passion, they *do* dig their graves with their teeth, they *are* devoured by ambition! The brutal and the unscrupulous may have the goods that we think would make us happy, but they are not made happy by them. In the quiet of my pastoral study, I have heard bullies cry that no one likes them, and liars weep because no one believes them, and pampered young people bitterly regretting that they were not taught self-control.

The virtues by which decent men live are not just goody-goody ways; they are not merely Puritanical prejudices; they are abiding spiritual goods which speak to the heart of man, which give rewards by themselves, whether or not they bring success, wealth, or power. And contrariwise, evil is real, and evil deeds bring their own punishment in their train. Hell is not a time; Hell is not a place; Hell is the condition of an evil heart.

And Heaven? What is Heaven like?

There is a lovely story from Jewish legend that describes it to a T. A pious man once fell asleep and dreamed this dream: An angel came and offered to show him all the mysteries of the universe. Eagerly he stood before the gates of Paradise, anxiously awaiting his first glimpse of the reward of the righteous. But how his mouth fell open when the gates swung apart. In Paradise he saw what looked very much like the little synagogue he had frequented on earth. And there in the pews were the saintly teachers and pious men who had been old men when he was a boy and now had departed the earth. They were sitting as they had on earth, before great folio volumes of Bible and Talmud, studying the word of the Lord. And as he looked, his face grew long, and in a puzzled and disappointed voice he asked the guiding angel, "Is *this* Heaven?" And the angel replied, "The righteous are not in Heaven, Heaven is in the righteous."

And so it surely must be. Heaven, whatever it is, cannot be so different from earth. Those values we cherish above all others, those pursuits which give life its truest meaning on earth, must surely be the stuff of which Heaven is made. When we are at our highest and best, in the presence of great beauty, in the study of great truths, in the doing of great deeds, then Heaven is in us, and what more could we desire in Heaven than this?

To wear a crown and strum a harp for all eternity has little challenge or meaning. But to go on sensing beauty, studying the great communications from God to man, and working for God's kingdom here and hereafter, what better Heaven could a man want?

The righteous are not in Heaven so much as Heaven is in the righteous.

II

Living with Yourself

1

Living with Wisdom

It has become something of a truism that man's technical skills have outpaced his moral controls. Almost every thinker of our time bemoans the gap between our scientific achievements and our ethical development. We have learned how to destroy the whole world before we have learned how to create one world.

But this is no new truth. Job called attention to it long ago. Go back and read Chapter 28: "There is a mine for silver and a place from which they take gold to refine. Man sets an end to darkness and searches in the deeps of the earth for brass and iron." And he goes on to describe the techniques and skills by which men mine the earth, going where no bird can fly nor lion walk, overturning mountains by the roots, and diverting creeks and rivers. All of this is within man's power. He can find the hidden silver, gold, and precious stones. And then, in a wistful voice, Job continues: "But wisdom, where is it to be found? Where is the location of understanding?"

To live well requires the development of intelligence, understanding, and wisdom.

Long ago, Hillel said that an ignorant man cannot be a good man. Our first reaction to such a statement is resentment. How can one even suggest that an ignorant person is incapable of goodness? What has character to do with knowledge? We know well-educated people who are wicked; why cannot ignorant people be good?

But experience has supported Hillel. An ignorant man does have a hard time being a good man. Good acts require skills and knowledge.

All of us would agree that an ignorant football player cannot be a good football player. Strong, co-ordinated, fleet he may be; but if he has not learned the signals nor studied the various plays, he will be useless to the team.

All of us would agree that an ignorant mechanic cannot be a good mechanic. Even with deft fingers and good tools, if he has not studied the subject, we would not entrust him with our television set or our automobile.

An ignorant man cannot be a good man unless he has learned the skills, acquired the knowledge necessary to doing what a good man wants to do.

From this point of view, the whole enterprise of education is reunited. We tend to divide education into skills and information on the one hand and character on the other. We forget that there can be no character without skills, and the things that we teach and the way we teach them imply a point of view and an ethic without our ever using the word. An ignorant man cannot be a good man.

This does not mean, of course, that every human being must have a degree after his name. This would be intellectual snobbery. But it does mean that every human being ought to add to his knowledge and his skills all his life. An uninformed voter cannot be a good voter; an uninformed citizen cannot be a good citizen; an ignorant man, even with the best intentions in the world, cannot be a good man unless he pursue knowledge and truth.

Make books your companions

To acquire the intelligence necessary to the good life requires learning, "book learning" as it is so often called. Books are vital to our life. They are the collective memory of our civilization. When the libraries of Rome and Greece were burned it was as though mankind developed amnesia. The accumulated wisdom of the past was destroyed and the Dark Ages began.

It was the rediscovery of books which led to the Renaissance, and with the invention of printing, knowledge became widespread. Instead of skills being handed down from father to son, instead of formulas being in the secret possession of family guilds, books made possible an accumulation of knowledge so that in each generation men could start where those before them had left off.

Rabbi Judah ibn Tibbon left an ethical will to his children in which he wrote: "Avoid bad society but make books your companions. Let your bookcases be your gardens. Pluck the fruit that grow therein, gather the roses. If your soul be weary, change from furrow to furrow. Then will your soul be satisfied with delight."

But as important as books and reading books may be, we need to understand the distinction between learning and wisdom.

Learning is the absorption of facts, the accretion of knowledge, the amassing of information, the development of skills. We learn to read, to write, to add and subtract. We learn the titles of Shakespeare's plays, or the advice of Polonius, or Hamlet's soliloquy. We learn the speed of light, and how to set off an atomic explosion. All of this is learning.

But wisdom is far more than learning. Wisdom is understanding. Wisdom is an insight into people's hearts, an intuitive grasp of a situation or problem, a long-range vision of what ought to be and a realistic assessment of what can be. In short, wisdom is a blend of the love of God with common sense.

Now there can be learning without wisdom. The Talmud describes this condition very cleverly.

"Unless a man clearly understands and inwardly digests what he studies, let him read ever so much; he can only be compared to a well-filled bookcase. Like a bookcase, he carries books within him, and like a bookcase, he is none the wiser for it."

But on the contrary, there can be little wisdom without learning. Learning is a tool of wisdom, and without tools wisdom will not achieve its purposes. I have met wise people who were uneducated, but never who were unlearned. Their wisdom was built on observation, on listening, on reading, and everything they had learned became grist for the mill of a wise intelligence which understood and digested whatever it had studied.

At school, our children are exposed to learning, to the reading of books and more books. They must also be taught to understand and digest what they study so that this learning may be distilled into wisdom.

Wisdom requires two very important qualities. The first of them is open-mindedness; the second is willingness to think.

The lesson of Galileo

The story of Galileo is an instructive lesson in the contrast between the open and the closed mind. We usually think of Galileo as a scientist, and his opponents as men of religion. We conclude, therefore, that scientists are men with minds open to new truths, whereas religionists are people whose minds are closed. What a surprise to discover, on reading de Santillana's *The Crime of Galileo,* that his first opponents were not religious officials at all, but scientists! Galileo invited those opponents to test his theories by looking through his telescope themselves, but some of those doctors of science *actually refused even to look.*

Open-mindedness is essential to wisdom, both scientific wisdom and religious wisdom.

Scientists are not all open-minded. Some of them were opposed to Pasteur and dismissed his theories as humbug; some of them dismissed Freud as a charlatan; some of them would not even look through Galileo's telescope.

Religionists are not all close-minded. New truths, new insights, new concepts have come in every age. The truly religious man says: "I will live by the truth as God gives me to see the truth." And he implies, as he says it, that if God gives him to see more truth, he will live by that.

The difference is not between religionists and scientists, but between those who believe they have all truth finally and forever and those who are at least willing to look through the telescope.

It is this which is a fundamental difference between democracy and totalitarianism. The very essence of our democratic faith is this: that no one man has all the truth, nor do all men have all the truth. Man's knowledge of what is best for him is incomplete; he can only act by the best that he knows while seeking a "better best." He is willing to look through the telescope; his mind is open. This is the way truth grows, this is the way a man grows, this is the way mankind grows.

The second characteristic of wisdom is a willingness to think.

A colleague of mine had finished a course in adult education at his Temple, and, seeking to improve his instruction, asked his "pupils" to evaluate the series, to tell what they liked about it and what they did not like.

One of the students wrote: "What I did *not* like was that your course made me think. I don't like to think."

I feel sure this was written tongue-in-cheek, and yet it reveals a widespread problem. We do not like to think! We do not like to think because thinking is work, hard work. If you do not think so, try it sometime.

As hard as it is to express clearly an idea you have, it is even harder to have an idea. The person who invented the phrase, "cudgel one's brain" was so right. Thinking is the hardest kind of work.

There is another reason we do not like to think. Thinking may lead us where we do not want to go. There was the man who said, "Don't confuse me with the facts; my mind is already made up." A lot of what we call thinking is simply the rearrangement of our existing attitudes. Real thought comes at a subject or a problem as though it were completely fresh, as though we had never thought about it nor felt anything toward it. And such thinking often leads down paths we do not want to travel; it upsets easy prejudgments and comfortable thoughts.

What a wonderful thing, then, when a minister, rabbi, or teacher can lead people to think, to re-examine the facts, and to re-think their conclusions from the facts. Out of such thoughts have come the works of genius, whether Einstein's theory or Shakespeare's poetry, and out of such thought has come the ability of men to recognize the truth of those theories and to enjoy that poetry.

As my colleague puts it, this is the answer to every teacher's prayer, to be able to make people think. For in this quality are we but little lower than the angels, by the power of intelligence do we become co-creators with God.

2

Living with Beauty

"I have never seen a spring so beautiful!" said a friend to me the other day. And I agreed. The wisteria have been more vivid, the branches of the redbud heavier with blossoms, the dogwood larger, the shoulders of the highways more flaming with color than I can remember ever before.

But, you know, I suddenly remember having this same conversation last year, and the year before that, and before that again. Every spring is the most beautiful, every spring is the loveliest yet. And why? Because each spring we have more memories of earlier springs, because our capacity to enjoy grows with our enjoyment, because our ability to recognize beauty grows with every exposure to it. This spring is more beautiful than last spring just because there was a spring last year.

And this is a lesson for all our lives. It is true of all the wonderful experiences we have.

So it is with love. When we fall in love, we think that never could two people love more deeply. But we do. Love is like spring—every year of it is more beautiful than the last. As Winston Churchill wrote of the Duke of Marlborough's life-long devotion to his wife: "Such a story of married love makes all the sizzling pictures of Purple Passion served up on the newsstands taste like ten cents' worth of cold potatoes."

So, too, with religious living, with brotherly love. Oh, that golden glow of doing a good deed! A child's face will shine with it; a Boy Scout takes pride in it; and as we mature, the joy of righteousness becomes deeper and richer; we earn the rewards of goodness in goodness itself.

This, I believe, is what Robert Browning had in mind when he put in the mouth of Rabbi ben Ezra: "Grow old along with me. The best is yet to be."

You say you never saw a spring so beautiful? Wait until next year!

What could be worse than for it not to come or not to be able to see it when it does?

Goethe records of one of his visits to Italy that up and down the street there were beggars holding out their hands for alms, but of them all, one seemed to be attracting the most attention. People might pass by one crippled beggar or another, but there was one whom no one seemed to overlook. And when Goethe came near, he saw why. On a sign this man had written:

IT IS APRIL AND I AM BLIND.

Never does spring come to Houston than I think of this story and of the pathos within it. How tragic it would be to be blind in Houston in the spring, not to be able to see the redbud like a mist against the sky, or the japonica's splashes of color against the winter-dulled grass, or the blaze of azaleas (surely this must have been Moses' burning bush). The beauty of spring is like no other beauty.

There is an awesome glory in a storm; sunsets have a peaceful beauty that is unmatched; the seas have a turbulent restless charm; but spring is beautiful as a baby is beautiful, spring is filled with tiny tender things.

Spring's beauty is purposeful, too. Some of nature's loveliness is more or less accidental. The Grand Canyon is the result of erosion, and mountains are heaved up by the earth in travail. But the new buds and flowers and the riot of spring's colors are a pattern of growth. The seed that sprouts has within it the beauty that is to be; the flower of spring is a harbinger of the fruit of fall. Spring's beauty is a living, developing beauty.

And most of all, spring's beauty leads to God. No other time of year reveals more perfectly His creative power. He is the divine Artist who scatters His flowers across the earth and makes the earth to bring forth beauty. The human heart, too, leaps with joy, and feeling spring in the air, and seeing it all about, feels all the more merciful to him who says: "It is April and I am blind."

How good to be alive in April. How good to see the spring and feel the presence of God.

Music can say more than words

Like the beauty of spring, the greatness of good music lies in the fact that each time you hear it, it becomes more beautiful. It is rather like the sort of melody that couples call "our song" which, for them, recalls a courtship and honeymoon. Great music does this for everyone; as it is heard again and again through the years, it accumulates associations that enrich its beauty.

This thought came again to mind when I last listened to Beethoven's Fifth. How many times have I heard that symphony? Fifty? A hundred? I have lost count, but I never hear it without its seeming more inspiring than before. As familiar as it is, it has never grown tiresome.

I can recall the first time I heard it high in the gallery of the symphony hall in Cincinnati. I was new to symphonic music in those days and did not enjoy much that I heard (as with olives, you have to develop a taste for it), but Beethoven's Fifth went right to my heart. I walked home in a cloud of splendor.

I bought a recording and played it over and over until its melodies became familiar and beloved friends. Through the years, it grew in beauty for me.

Then, after serving as chaplain overseas for almost eighteen months without the opportunity of listening to music, I attended a concert in Manila. It was given in a church—a bombed church without a roof, with rubble still piled about it. Little lights twinkled overhead. Then suddenly from the orchestra came those magnificent opening notes. I sat there that night and cried without shame. Everything for which we had been fighting was somehow summed up in that music.

And so it has been ever since. Each time I hear Beethoven's Fifth, these and many more memories add to its beauty.

Popular music is enjoyable. You can sing it, dance to it; but it comes and goes. This week's top melody is next week's tired tune. But great music is music that lasts, it is music to grow by, music to live by.

Even more, music can sometimes say what words cannot convey.

This thought is emphasized by a beautiful rabbinic story. The Rabbi of Lodi was a great preacher. He had an intellect which could put great thoughts in clear and forceful language, along with an eloquence which gave to his language a high emotional charge. One Sabbath this wise and eloquent rabbi was delivering an impassioned discourse in the synagogue when he noticed that one old man was straining to understand his words. His face was puzzled and bewildered as he tried to follow the trend of the rabbi's discourse.

After the services were over, the rabbi went up to the old gentleman and said: "I could see by the expression on your face that you did not understand my sermon."

"This is true," said the old man, somewhat ashamed.

"Then it must have been my fault," said the rabbi. "Let me try again." And he threw back his head, closed his eyes, and sang with real ecstasy a song without words, a pure melody so expressive of faith and of longing that the old man's face lit up like the sunrise as understanding dawned in his heart.

Music can sometimes say what words cannot convey.

Actually, I suppose we all have known this without ever thinking about it. You can listen to a folk song, a lullaby, or an aria in some foreign language and you do not have to be told what the words say. The music says it, sadly or gladly, lovingly or angrily. This is equally true of a Hebrew chant. Few know the words of the Day of Atonement's *Kol Nidre*, but the melody is loved by millions.

Do you know the words to our national anthem? Actually, it begins with a long and complicated sentence: "O say, can you see by the dawn's early light what so proudly we hailed at the twilight's last gleaming?" That is a mouthful of words, and if you did not know what was coming next, you would not know whether he was talking about a fort or a flag or both. But it really does not make any difference. It is the melody which we hear, which we love, and which arouses our love for America and our appreciation of freedom. If all we did was hum it, we would still know what it meant without a word's being sung.

Yes, music can say so much that words cannot convey about man and about God.

Creation is difficult, destruction easy

Beauty in nature is of God's making; beauty in art, architecture, and music is of man's doing. Beauty of all sorts is the result of creation, God's and man's. And it is a curious paradox of human life that building should take so long, and destroying takes so little time; that creation should be difficult and destruction so easy; but, despite this truth, that the forces of creation should prevail.

I recall reading a beautiful article on this subject. Construction and creation are long and difficult to achieve; destruction is immediate and easy. A human being takes nine months to form in the womb, and years of care and education to be matured for self-directed living. How much effort and how much of an investment! A mother's love, a father's care, a community's concern with schools and colleges, all to build a single human being—and yet how easily that life can be snuffed out. A squeal of brakes and the body is broken; the invasion of a virulent microbe, and fever burns it up; the spat of a bullet across no man's land, and life is gone. Creation is difficult; destruction is easy.

They took a long time building a great ship. Steel and wood were fabricated with care, put together by workmen trained for years in the arts of shipbuilding; huge sums of money were invested, and finally the *Titanic* was launched for trans-Atlantic sailing. Years of effort to build, then just a moment of collision with an iceberg and all the creative labor went to the bottom of the sea. Creation is difficult; destruction is easy.

A library was assembled in ancient times in Egypt. Each book was the product of a mind that had labored over ideas and poured out effort to put those ideas on paper. Each book was laboriously copied by hand, catalogued, and put in place—the creative treasures of man's search for truth. Then some barbaric fools came and set it to the torch and in ten minutes the intellectual achievement of centuries went up in smoke. Creation is difficult; destruction is easy.

My congregation has an unusually beautiful Temple. It was five years in the creating. It began as an idea in the mind of an architect, was worked out on the drawing board after consultation with engineers of many sorts, experts in steel structure, masonry, plumbing, acoustics. The whole range of building skills was called upon, the finest mechanics were employed, each piece of wood was sawed, sanded, finished, and put in place. Every detail of that building was the result of hours of thought and labor. In money terms it cost over $750,000. One day, watching some men demolish a building, I asked the superintendent to estimate how much it would cost to demolish our Temple. "About $50,000," he replied. Creation is difficult; destruction is easy.

Everything in this world, everything which is the product of creative mind and skilled labor, is at the mercy and the whim of the destructive forces, accidents, brute force, microbes, fire, earthquake, cyclone, death. All take their toll.

And yet, in the perspective of time, the creative forces are winning out. Not because they work faster—creation is slow, destruction is fast—but because construction has a purpose while destruction has none. Creation involves foresight, thoughtfulness, method, co-operation. Creation is going some place. Destruction is meaningless, purposeless, random. It goes no place.

Lightning is not out to destroy the tree, but the tree is out to grow tall toward the sky. The careless smoker's cigarette does not think how it can burn down a house, but the builder gives his whole being to the raising of a dwelling.

The world itself, you see, is not random accident but the work of an Intelligence with Purpose. The only time God destroyed was by the flood, and that only to start the process of creation over again. Creative activity, construction, is allied with every deep force and purpose in the universe, so even though destruction is easy and takes little time, it cannot win because it runs counter to the very fiber of life.

Therefore, those who would walk with God will create, not destroy. We shall bring children into the world and do our best to raise them to mature human beings. We shall plan homes and houses of worship. We shall join creative efforts to bring men and nations together in fellowship and in peace because we know that "He who daily renewest the work of Creation" is on our side, that the future belongs to those who create.

Living for Growth

Growth is a law of life. What does not grow is dead or dying. This is true biologically, and it is true spiritually.

We can learn a lesson in growth from a tree trunk. If you look at the trunk of a freshly cut tree you will see a series of concentric circles—the rings of the tree. Each of those rings represents a year's growth. Count them and you will know the age of the tree. More than this, by measuring the rings, we can measure the rainfall. Weather cycles of long ago are revealed in the rings of very old trees. Thin rings indicate dry seasons, thick rings point to heavy rainfall.

There are no rings in the human trunk, but physicians claim that in a post-mortem operation, they can find evidences of every disease a person ever had. Every vitamin deficiency, every accident and illness leave their ineradicable mark upon the body. A skilled pathologist can find the signs of diseases of long years past, measles, mumps, pneumonia, or liver trouble. The body, like a tree trunk, carries within it the record of its years.

And what is true of a tree and of a body is likewise true of a character, a heart, a soul. Psychologists and psychiatrists can plot out the emotional weather of our earlier years, whether there was too little sunshine of affection, too little rainfall of approval. Our childhood triumphs and defeats, loves and hates, mark us for life, and leave their traces on the soul.

Three ways to measure your growth

But there is one difference in our analogies. A tree cannot measure its own age. The body cannot perform its own post mortem, but the living, growing human being can measure its own growth of soul, its own achievement of character. Sometimes we may need the help of psychiatrists to achieve insight, but most of the time we can measure our own growth, most of the time we can, if we will, know ourselves.

The Talmud suggests a triple battery of tests for insight both into other human beings and for self-knowledge. In the Hebrew, these three clues are alliterative. In English, they lose their poetry but not their truth. A man's true nature is revealed, the Talmud says, by three things, *koso, kahso,* and *kiso,* when he is in his cups, by his temper, and by his purse. Now this means more than that a man is most truly himself when he is drunk or angry or arguing about money. It means more than this. It means that a man's growth, his maturity, may be measured by the way he handles his liquor, his temper, and his wealth.

Surely one of the great problems of our time is alcoholism. The smash-up of automobiles and the smash-up of family lives are so often due to this very cause. We have learned that alcoholism is a disease, an illness of the personality, a way of escape from life's problems. It is not alcohol which is the problem but a man's inability to handle life's frustrations without resorting to the cup. And certainly Judaism has a lot to teach on this subject. We have long used wine to gladden the heart in the ceremony that leads to the Sabbath, to a holy day, to a marriage. But we have learned temperance as well. On the Passover, the observant celebrant will drink the required four cups of wine, but the fifth cup which is for Elijah he leaves strictly alone. Alcohol is good for relaxation, it is bad if it is for escape. A man is measured *b'koso,* by his cup.

By *kahso* as well. A man is measured by his control of his

temper. There is nothing more characteristic of little children than their outbursts. They have little control. The smallest interference with them and the heavens are brought down by their screaming anger. There is nothing more character- istic of the childish in men and women than this display of temper. Maturity implies control in two ways: a control of the temper that does arise, and a maturity in which less tem- per rises. In *The Ethics of the Fathers* we read of the anger from the most miserable, which is quick to be aroused and slow to appease, to the happiest, which is slow to rise and quick to subside. Surely maturing should mark progress from one to the other. There was a rabbi once, who, when he felt temper rising within him, would proceed to look up the books of religious ethics on whether he was permitted to express that anger. I feel sure he banged his books as he looked, but by the time he discovered the law, how much anger could he have had left?

But even more than controlling our outbursts, we have to learn not to be irritated, to be patient with people, to be less concerned with our own status. There are times for anger, for righteous indignation, but a real man is measured by the way he controls his temper.

But above all, a man is measured by his *kiso*, by his purse. Philip Guedalla, the biographer, once wrote that he had done research on the life of the Duke of Wellington for many months, yet felt he had not yet captured the man's personal- ity—did not know him. "Then," he wrote, "I came across some account books of the Iron Duke that told me how he spent his money for several years. And reading those dry figures, I came to know him." A man is known by his purse, because the ways he spends his money reveals the way he thinks and the values he holds.

Think about this a moment! The things you spend money on reveal the things you believe in, the things you put first and the things you put last. Many a man has a charitable mouth and a tight purse, a religious air and an irreligious pocketbook.

Some people believe in the appearance of things—they put most into clothes, cars, homes, flashy things where the money shows. Others believe in security above all else, and will live meanly and in foolish self-denial for some tomorrow they may never enjoy. Some believe in pandering to their appetites and all their money goes for food; others have no thought except for fun, and will put an outboard motor before another expenditure.

Man is known by his *kiso*, his purse. What do you believe in? Do not ask yourself and then answer—just consult your check stubs. Man is known by his purse.

These then are the measure of a man, as delightfully suggested in the *bon mot* of an ancient rabbi: *b'koso, b'kiso, uv'kahso.* A man is known to other men, to himself, even to God, by his cup, by his purse, and by his anger.

Spiritual growth demands an increasing ability to handle our desires, our tempers, and our income.

Weeds spring up by themselves

When we are young, we depend on our parents to provide the proper food for our physical health and growth. When we are mature, we must watch our own diets. Likewise, in our childhood our parents and teachers must nourish us spiritually, and in our maturity we must provide our own soul's food. Because growth must be directed.

We might take a lesson from nature. I have seen our lawn turn brown while right in the middle of it the weeds are as green as can be. Our rose bushes will droop, but the milkweed stands straight and strong. Why?

Apparently this has been going on a long time. In Talmudic days, Rabbi Chanina ben Pazzi said, "Weeds spring up by themselves but to produce wheat takes much time and trouble."

And when you come to think about it, you can find an

answer. Weeds have no purpose except to be weeds. They have nothing else to do but grow strong and reproduce. But domestic plants are designed for a larger purpose, to give food, or to add beauty to life. The purposeless is easy, the purposeful takes effort. Weeds grow without care; wheat takes trouble.

The same thing is true of human character.

Human weeds spring up by themselves; human wheat takes time and effort. We can develop bad habits without half trying. Out of the natural soil of envy and gluttony, there grow weeds of character that will choke out every flower. But if we would develop the beauty of virtue, then we must dig, plant, and water.

So, too, with our children. Let them run wild, ignore them, neglect them, and they will grow into weeds. To help them flower into beautiful lives takes constant cultivation, love's sunlight, the living waters of learning, the weeding out of bad attitudes. Parents must be the devoted gardeners of growing children.

And all of us, whether parents or not, have an obligation to provide a good soil for all our community's children. It is easy for children to become delinquents in slums and on crowded streets. We must provide them with playgrounds and playtime guidance if we would have them grow into good citizens. For weeds spring up by themselves, but to produce wheat takes time and trouble.

Jumping off the diving board

Growth can be directed to a certain point by parents, teachers, and recreation leaders, but ultimately a human being must move from being directed to self-direction.

This was brought home to me by a very amusing story told by a Red Cross swimming instructor.

A little boy came home in high excitement. "Daddy! Mother!" he shouted, "I jumped off the high diving board!"

"But son," his parents interjected, "that's what you told us last week."

The boy answered quickly, "But this time no one pushed me!"

Isn't that life? We give our children piano lessons, dancing lessons, tuba lessons, and we stand over them like Simon Legrees: Practice! Practice! (Do you suppose Van Cliburn's mother did that?) And then one day they go from practicing only when nagged to practicing for fun. What a day that is!

Parents push a boy to study in high school. Every night they remind him of his lessons and are so proud if he makes A's. Then off he goes to college, and if he makes A's this time they can be even prouder because no one pushed him.

Growing up is this process. Maturity means that we have moved from being pushed to pushing ourselves, from being motivated to self-motivation. And this applies not only to skills but also to ethics.

Early in life we tell the truth because, perhaps, we are afraid to lie. One day we learn to love the truth for its own sake.

Early in life, we give because everyone else is giving, and we do not want to seem stingy. One day we learn to give out of compassion.

Early in life, we go to worship services because Mother and Dad take us. At maturity, we learn to love our faith for its own sake.

When we are childish in faith, we do good because we fear hell or would earn heaven. If we mature, no one has to push us, we do good for God's sake and would help build heaven on earth.

Nor should that developing maturity, that spiritual growth ever cease. I was appalled to read this quotation from Fran-çoise Sagan, the young French novelist: "At nineteen, I could have been changed, but now I can no longer change the set of reflexes which is me."

There is something both amusing and tragic about these

words. Amusing because when she wrote those words, Fran-
çoise Sagan was still only twenty-four. Tragic because a
young woman with a life expectancy of forty or fifty more
years claims she is no longer capable of growth.

Unfortunately, too many people agree with her, and believe that only in youth are we flexible, that maturity means
fixed reflexes.

It would be a terrible thing if this were so, and of course,
if we believe it, we make it so. We have unfortunately been
bemused and misled by our inadequate understanding of
the findings of psychology and psychiatry. We think of ourselves as entirely the products of our childhood, as puppets
of the past, with Oedipus and Electra and libido and id pull-
ing the strings. And so we conceive of ourselves as being
powerless to effect changes in our reactions and behavior.
With maturity, we can no longer change "the set of reflexes
which is me."

But we fail to follow through. Psychology does not end
with this insight into the unconscious causes of our behavior
patterns. It goes on to suggest a cure, which is to free ourselves of the puppet strings. Maturity does not mean we become fixed and set; rather does it mean becoming aware of
ourselves and our reflexes, so that our behavior is no longer
the product of reflexes but of reflection, of thought, and of
will.

Psychiatry and religion meet at the point where the Bible
says: "Behold, I set before you this day good and evil, and
life and death. Now choose."

Men are capable of change, and women as well, even
Françoise Sagan. People can remold their own outlook and
characters, not only at nineteen but at twenty-nine and sixty-
nine. Real character, and real joy in life, is to be found in the
flexibility of the spirit, in the growth of the soul.

Learn from the mountain climbers

In seeking the higher peaks of character, we would do well to
follow the advice of mountain climbers. In going up a steep

slope, do not look down, and while climbing, do not look far up ahead, but rather to the points close by. Because if you look down while climbing a steep slope, it is easy to get dizzy, perhaps even to lose your footing. And if you look constantly at the peaks above you, you will get discouraged by how little progress you make from step to step. Better rather to stop for breath now and then. Then you can look down to see how far you have really come and feel good about it before you look up once more to the peaks you seek to climb.

Now I do not know how good this advice is to mountain climbers. I read it someplace, and have not tried it out. But I do know what good advice it is for life, and for climbing the mountainsides of character and for straining to reach the peaks of achievement. Either looking down or looking up as you climb is a risky business. Only while taking a breather should one look to other than the immediate step ahead.

If you look down a steep slope, it is so easy to get dizzy, frightened, or both. If you think how easy it would be to fall, to lose your job, to flunk a course, to make a bust of things you aspire to, then you are likely to fail. A man in business told me that once he was in a very perilous position, like a man on a tightrope. He had overextended himself, and one false move, one bad week, and he would be bankrupt. "But," he said, "I refused to think about it. I only tried to do what I had to do each day and each hour of the day, for I knew if I did not lose my head I would make it."

A young boy going overseas in our division came to me with his fears. "I don't see how I'll ever get back alive," he kept saying. "If I get through one action alive, then I'll have to go out again, and again and again, and sooner or later I'm sure to get it." He kept looking downhill, you see, and became frightened. And I had to keep reassuring him that he did not have to think about nor worry about the "again and again," that if he did and lost his nerve, he would be killed in combat sooner—that only a cool head, and a resolve just to do what was on hand to be done and not to worry about the next step until it was at hand would keep him alive.

If you look down the chasm and see what awful things might happen, if you worry over the slips you might make, the dangers that lurk around the corner, you cannot climb the mountains of life.

And likewise, if you look constantly toward the peaks, you are likely to fail because they are so far away, and no sooner have you climbed one than a larger one looms ahead. I have never climbed a mountain—only some small foothills, and even then I discovered how true this is. You look up, then huff and puff and climb till you are just exhausted, then look up and it looks as though you have made no headway at all; the top seems just as far as before.

And isn't that so in life as well? A young man decides to be a doctor. It's a long, long climb—college, medical school, in-terne, resident—ten years at least, twelve years for many, and if each day of your first year you say, "Still twelve years, still twelve years, still twelve years," you will never make it—never. A woman begins to raise a family, and it takes more than twelve years—many more. There are thou-sands of diapers to be washed, millions of dishes to be dried, years and years of care, worry, car pools, children's fool-ishness and tears. Why, if you think about it all at once, it's just too much.

So don't look up so much, but undertake each day's task, and do each hour's work, and climb step by step up the mountainside of achievement, and then one day, before you know it, there you are at the top!

Of course, there are times to stop, to stop and look up, to get your bearings and be sure you have stayed on the right mountainside, and are still aimed toward the peak. There are times when a person should stop for a few moments of medi-tation to renew his vision of the peaks toward which he climbs, to enjoy the beauty of the way and enjoy the satisfac-tion of seeing how far he has really come. Then, in his house of worship, he will sit and contemplate the mountains whence our help comes, and rededicate himself to the way that leads ever upwards to our God. Then, from his house of worship, he will renew the climb, looking neither down nor up, but taking each step after dedicated step toward the peaks of his life's goal.

Growth cannot be steady

There is another warning we need, we who would grow in character. We need to realize that growth is not steady. As the rings in a tree trunk reveal, there are years of plentiful rainfall and years of drought. In the development of character, we sometimes even slip backwards. We set goals and fail them, we make resolutions and break them.

I can remember how seriously I used to take the writing of New Year's resolutions when I was a boy. I would sit down very solemnly to make my list: to help mother without grumbling, to keep my clothes and room neat, not to hit my little brother, to keep my temper, to go to bed early, and so forth. Yes, it was a solemn and serious business.

I can remember, too, wondering why it was, if everybody made so many wonderful resolutions, that the world was not a much better place after New Year's than before. I was just a boy, I could not be expected to live up perfectly to everything I promised; but grown people, I thought, had perfect control, and once they resolved, it would be done—at least for a long time, and if the resolutions wore down, it would only be toward the end of the year. Why, when so many pious promises were being made, and why was it that the world did not immediately become a happier and sweeter place?

But then as I grew older, I came to understand people better, myself included. I began to realize how easy it is to make good resolutions and how hard it is to keep them.

I would sit in a symphony concert, and if the music inspired me, I would begin to dream grand dreams about my life. In a world, I would think to myself, in which there is so much beauty, so much wonder, such incomparable music, how can a person live anything but an exalted life? How can a person be concerned with petty matters and little things? How can a person lose his temper, fly off the handle, sulk, or go off in a peeve? The world is too wonderful for such things.

And, the concert over, I would walk out on cloud 9. But while driving out of the parking lot, someone would cut in on me and take unfair advantage of me, and then—well, you know how it is.

It is easy to make resolutions in a dreamy mood away from the traffic, but to live in the middle of life's snarled highways—this takes a lot more.

It is rather like the experience most parents have. A father comes home in the evening, weary, exhausted from the day's labors. His wife is tired too from a day of housekeeping and child-minding. The only ones who aren't tired are the children. They are energetic, boisterous, bubbling. So much so that they wear on the nerves, they frazzle the patience. Their voices hurt the ear, their squabbling rends the evening, and gradually a father's temper frays, his voice is lifted, and his hand, too. By the time the children are all in bed and quieted down, and the last giggle has sounded and the last glass of water has been drunk, parents are "fit to be tied."

But an hour or two later, when bedtime has come, and the parents go in to check on the little ones, there they lie on their pillows—little faces like angels, their hair like a halo, so peaceful, so quiet, so darling. Then the conscience begins to smite: "How can we be so impatient?" a mother and father ask each other. "What do we expect from just children? Why shouldn't they make noise? It's their home, too. Really, we are too intolerant, too bad-tempered. We have to be patient and loving and sweet and understanding." And it gets to the point where father says, "I'm going to turn over a new leaf. I'm going to treat them as children. I am never going to lose my temper again!"

And on that high note of resolve, off mother and father go to bed.

But then, at six-thirty in the morning, little fingers pry open an eyelid, and a little voice shrieks, "Daddy, are you in there yet?" and it starts all over again!

It's not too difficult to keep those promises we make to ourselves about ourselves. Most people I know who swear off smoking actually do quit. But the promises we make to ourselves about our relationship to others—ah, this is a different matter. Perhaps we can control our temper with inanimate things, be more self-controlled when we stumble over a chair, run into a door, or hit our finger with a hammer. But when people annoy us, when cars cut in on us, when children wear us out, this is a different thing.

And yet we ought not to stop making resolutions. "A man's reach should exceed his grasp, or what's a Heaven for?" Perhaps we cannot succeed in all our dreams of self-improvement. Life is a continual struggle for growth, but dream we ought, and dream we must, or all will be lost.

We grow or we die, both physically and spiritually.

4

The Conquest of Self

It must be a lot easier to be an animal than a human being. All an animal has to do is adapt to nature around him. A human being must also conquer nature within him. An animal can, to the extent of its strength, satisfy its hungers and express its passions freely. A human being must learn to say no to his hunger, passions, and ambitions. And of all man's achievements, this is the most difficult.

A Talmudic story illustrates this truth. Alexander the Great, it is related, came to the gates of Paradise, knocked imperiously and demanded admittance.

"You cannot come in here," said a voice from within.

"But this is Alexander," he shouted, "Alexander the Great, Alexander the master of the earth, Alexander the conqueror."

"Only one conqueror is admitted here," the voice replied, "and it is he who has conquered himself."

Of all man's conquests, this is the most difficult and also the most vital. We live in an age in which this has become the most important of all man's tasks. We have fulfilled God's command to Adam to subdue the earth and rule it. We have subdued the earth and harnessed its enormous power, but God's command to Cain, "Sin coucheth at the door but thou mayest prevail," we have not fulfilled.

In fact, the word "sin" has almost disappeared from our vocabulary. Very few people speak any more about sin, or refer to people as sinners. You can read the newspaper editorials, or the true confessions magazines; you can go to movies or see plays; the word "sin" has almost disappeared. It is virtually a lost word.

It is not only a lost word but a lost concept. With it has gone a whole pattern of moral judgments and moral standards of which it was a part. It is not merely that people are breaking the law, the law of the land or the law of God. It is not merely that the taxpayer has falsified his tax return, or the judge perverted justice, or the policeman broken the law—it is that we the people seem to have become indifferent; we overlook it, expect it, participate in it. Sin is a lost word.

How have we lost this word, and the moral standards it represents?

Part of our loss is due to an exaggerated reaction to English Victorianism and Puritanical standards. We are still in revolt against a system of behavior which intertwined morals and manners and made virtures out of mere proprieties. In yesterday's world, we parody, nice people had good morals *and* good manners. If you did not have good manners, you were not nice people. But today, we have almost decreed that nice people need have neither morals NOR manners, as long as they are interesting. In this school of thought, the word "sin" is so puritanical, so old-fashioned. Bring up sin, and you will be told, "Really, fellow, don't be stuffy."

Another cause of our loss of the word is our exaggerated reaction to the psychology of a few years ago, a misunderstanding of what the new science of human behavior had to contribute to human life. Moral scruples became inhibitions. People were no longer sinners, they were just maladjusted. To spank your children was denounced as a cause of psychological trauma, and a whole generation grew up taught to free themselves of psychological blocks, to do what they wanted to do. Though this was, of course, started by responsible psychologists, it was exaggerated by the amateur, the enthusiastic laymen who sought an excuse to evade high moral standards.

And then we lost the word "sin" in the moral relativities laid bare by the anthropologists who explored various societies in the present world and in the past and found differing customs in differing lands and ages. The logical conclusion seemed to be that if morals differ from land to land and from generation to generation, how can we then speak of right and wrong as immutable standards? People are the creatures of their time and place. In a world in which economic success becomes a powerful drive, the corrupt public official is no longer a thief, but a pitiful victim of this economic situation. And the Kinsey Reports suggested that we really ought to change our sex laws to conform to human behavior rather than change our behavior to conform to morals.

But morals, real morals, do not change. Fashions change, manners change, moral principles do not. And the mere fact that people do something or have done something or would like to do something in large masses does not make it good or right. The Ten Commandments were not written on sand but on rock, intended to endure. Moral relativity will never go so far as to say: "Thou shalt murder." Far from it! The direction is the other way. We are getting away even from those forms of murder (like the death penalty and war) which have been sanctioned in the past. We shall never say: "Thou shalt steal." We shall never believe in false witness, in adultery. Moral principles are not so easily abandoned.

Modern psychology has brought great gains in understanding human personality, helped deal with the wayward and the lost, but, if we understand it well, it has reinforced, not weakened, morality. It has proved by scientific research what religion has taught for a long time: that sin and a sense of guilt are enemies of human personality, enemies of human happiness.

We need to recover the word "sin," and having recovered it, seek to conquer it.

Sailing across the wind

To conquer ourselves requires self-discipline.

In 1944, when the army battalion of which I was chaplain was in Milne Bay, New Guinea, for training, many of us spent our leisure hours on the water. And for the first time in my life I learned something about boats. A friend and I purchased an outrigger canoe from one of the natives, and then would paddle ourselves from island to island in the bay. But paddling was hard work, and so we decided to put a sail and a rudder on our boat. We took long strong sticks of bamboo and attached a large piece of canvas, then we took a broom stick and used the end of an apple box for a rudder. Now, we thought, we are ready to go sailing, and a-sailing we did go. Whenever we went the same way the wind went, it was really wonderful. We skimmed along the water. But then we tried to go across the wind. We set our sail at a forty-five-degree angle to the wind, and our boat at ninety degrees. We moved, but we moved in a way we had not anticipated. We moved downward at the same time we moved across wind, so that if the wind were coming from the west and we set our sails to go north, we actually went northeast, and more east than north.

We looked for someone who could tell us what was wrong. We found a soldier who had sailed boats on Lake Michigan, and after he looked our boat over, he told us that our boat was sideslipping. It rode so high in the water that the same wind that was supposed to drive us forward was also moving us sideward. What we needed was a keel. All we had to do was to get a good-sized board and fix it vertically to the bottom of the boat. A keel would give us a good grip on the water and let us go forward without sideslipping.

Thus we learned something about sailing. But it seems to me that we also learned something about life and about character.

In the voyage across the seas of life, all of us need both

sail and keel. We need the forward thrust of the sail that will get us places, but we also need the restraining influence of the keel that will keep us on our course.

The wind in our life is our energy, our ambition, our drive. The desire to grow, to accomplish, to achieve is what gives us our forward thrust; it impels us toward our goal.

But without restraint, that energy and that drive are subject to sideslip. Instead of getting where we intended, we go off in many directions. We follow one ambition, and then another, take one course of studies leading to one goal, and then in midterm decide we did not want that at all. We join a multitude of clubs and organizations and give none of them our full attention. We sideslip and lose half, or more than half, the results of our energy.

Our lives need keels. Our lives need keels that go down deep into the water, and keep the ship of which we are master straight on its course.

That keel is discipline, self-discipline, the channeling of our energies and our ambitions into constructive paths. We customarily think of discipline as a negative thing, "don't do this and don't do that," but discipline is positive. A football player may keep training by not smoking, by not staying up late, by not overeating, but these do not make him a football player. What makes him a football player is what he does: exercise, practice, training, discipline.

And so with all of us. Character is not the denial of life but the control of life. Character is not the suppression of energies but the control of energies. Character resides far more in what we do than in what we avoid doing. The boats of our lives need both sail and keel, the energy of our bodies, and the control of our souls.

To conquer ourselves by self-discipline also requires a projected self-image of high idealism.

This is suggested by Max Beerbohm's fairy tale, *The Happy Hypocrite:*

Once upon a time there was a wicked, wicked man. His

name was Lord George Hell, and his character was as black
as his name. But not only did he have an evil heart, he had
an evil face. He not only was a villain, but he looked like a
villain. People would blanch with terror when he entered
a room. Children would run from him screaming. He was
not just ugly, he was evil to look upon.

Now Lord George Hell fell in love. He fell in love with a
sweet and beautiful and innocent maiden, and he proposed
to her. But she refused him. She would not, she said, marry
a man unless he had the face of a saint. So Lord George Hell
went to the cleverest mask maker in the world, and paid
him a fabulous sum of money to make him a mask that he
might wear, a mask of a saintly man. The mask was made and
fitted to his face so carefully that none could recognize that
it was artificial.

Now with his new face, Lord George Hell again wooed
the maiden whom he loved. She accepted him and they were
married. But even after they were married she did not learn
the truth. For he struggled to control his evil, checked his
wicked impulses, treated her with consideration and kindness, and in all ways acted the part his mask called for. They
were very happy, Lord Hell and his young bride, and the
years went by. But then one day one of his enemies found
him out, and in the presence of his wife, proceeded to tear
the mask from Lord Hell's face. But lo and behold, when the
mask was gone, there was no change. The old face of evil
had disappeared; beneath the mask of a saint there now appeared the face of a saint. And they lived happily forever
after.

Max Beerbohm, in this little fairy tale, had hold of a
mighty truth. Two mighty truths, as a matter of fact. One of
them has to do with our near and dear ones, the other with
all our life.

For here we see the power of love, and what love can
do to change the face and behind the face, the heart of a
human being. Isn't it true that when we love, we change

our ways? A carefree, heedless, irresponsible boy falls in love, and turns into a thoughtful and considerate head of a household. A girl whose days might seem to be one round of pleasure-seeking foolishness bears a child and becomes in all ways a mother. I have seen men come out of prison, and, under the spell of love for a good woman, become upstanding, righteous citizens. It is love that calls forth the qualities of tenderness, respect, and duty. For our loved ones we do what we would never have dreamed ourselves capable of. And over the years of self-control, we develop new and deeper character, finer and higher sensibilities. We grow through loving.

And then, from a broader point of view, this fairy tale tells us something about life. For all of us are hypocrites, at least a little bit. None of us shows his full face to the world. We take part in activities in which we really have little interest; we support causes because it's the thing to do. When we would like to scowl, we smile; when we would rather strike out, we are polite. And sometimes we are ashamed that our inner feelings do not correspond to our outer acts. Perhaps someone asks a sacrifice of us. We make the sacrifice, but inside we grudge it. And we ask ourselves, why can't I feel good when I do good? Why can't I do this gladly? And thus we create a tension within us, and feel that while the face we show the world is a good face, the face we show God is a bad face. We want to be whole and sound, not divided and unsound. We do not like hypocrisy in ourselves.

Yet, at least this is what it seems to me Max Beerbohm's fairy tale tells us, our hearts do grow to reflect our outer actions. If we control what we feel, and do what we know to be just and right and good, then somehow our inner countenance begins to look like our outer appearance. We become saints by acting saintly.

Surely this gives us courage. There is no man living who has a perfect heart. But if he will guide his actions by demands of love, then he will increasingly prevail.

Admit you have been wrong

To conquer oneself also requires confession of failure. It is rare that a human being will publicly admit to wrong. Our consciences may stab us privately, but publicly we bluster with self-justification. Any parent can tell you that the hardest thing to teach a child to say is, "I'm sorry," and if we be honest with ourselves, we adults find it equally difficult. Somehow to admit having done wrong seems to bruise our ego and threaten our self-respect.

How refreshing, therefore, is this story from a recent book, *Tears and Laughter in an Israel Courtroom* by Judge Shneour Z. Cheshin:

A certain judge in Jerusalem was widely known for his hot temper. Even in the courtroom he would insult those who angered him. One day a plaintiff appeared in his court who displeased the judge. She was heavily made up and wore loud clothes. After she had given her testimony, the judge glared at her. "I do not believe a single word of your lies. Your ways are the ways of a streetwalker!"

"Your honor," said the woman, "in a court of law all are equal, great or small, rich or poor. What a man or woman does outside the courthouse must not influence the scales of justice. I came to this court because it is a fountainhead of impartial justice. Instead, you have publicly shamed me."

The crowd held its breath. They expected a storm of abuse.

But instead, the judge, his head bowed in shame, stood up, went from his bench to the dock where the accused stand, dictated a complaint against himself, found himself guilty, and paid his fine.

What a magnificent lesson for life! Real character involves not only the desire and the capacity to live by high ideals, it also includes the ability to say, "I have sinned," to say it not only in the privacy of the heart but in public as well.

But above all, the conquest of self requires an almost abandoned embrace of virtue. If we fill our lives with affirmations,

we will have no time for negatives; if we use our time for
good it will crowd out the evil.

There are things in life which we ought not to calculate
carefully but to which we ought to give ourselves unre-
servedly and wholeheartedly.

The Talmud teaches this lesson. At the end of a chapter
which deals with various religious and ethical obligations such
as the size of a sacrifice, the specifications for first fruits, the
monetary value of peace offerings, and so forth, there is this
sentence: "The following are things for which there is *no*
measure: the corner of the field left for the poor, the free-will
offering to God, the study of the Bible, the deeds of loving-
kindness."

The implications of this are very plain. There are some
areas in life in which our obligations are quite precise and
measurable; if we perform these duties carefully, we are
acquitted of our debts to society. But there are other areas in
which, if we begin by asking how much or how often, we lose
the spirit of righteousness. If we give to the poor with a calculating hand, if we seek to get just "passing" grades, if we
perform our good deeds in only measured quantity, we are,
according to the Talmud, losing the savor of good living.
Some part of our lives ought to be spent with a lavish hand.

The same principle might easily be applied to our times.
Would any one set limits to the obligations of citizenship?
Do you recall the racketeer who said he was a good American, he paid his taxes and voted at every election? If patriot-
ism is ever "measured out" it will no longer be true love of
fatherland.

And above all, this principle would apply to family life.
All talk about marriage being a fifty-fifty proposition is mis-
leading. It implies that both husband and wife begin to "keep
records"; that if one "gets ahead of the other" their marriage
has been unsuccessful. How foolish! And how easy for a marriage, based on such mathematical give-and-take, to go sour.

Only if love is given generously and without concern for "returns" can there be a truly happy marriage.

There are some things we may count. But the important things, the Talmud tells us, are limitless.

Moreover, people often make distinctions between the large virtues and the little kindnesses, between gross sins and small faults. And frequently we excuse our lesser failings by pointing to our greater good. A husband, defending his discourtesy or thoughtlessness, will piously remind his wife that he always brings home his paycheck, and never gets drunk. A wife, accused of nagging, will point to her virtues as cook or mother. A youth will neglect the development of social graces with a shrugged "Why should I bother with good manners; let them learn to know the 'real me.'"

The Talmudic sages warned against making such distinctions. They pointed out that man cannot know what is ultimately most important—the small virtues are just as important as the large.

For example, they called attention to two Biblical commandments. One of them was a great principle: "Honor your father and your mother." The other called only for a small kindness: "When you stumble upon a nest, and a mother bird brooding over eggs, you may take the eggs, but not the dam." In man's eyes these statutes are not equivalent. One requires a lifetime to observe, the other is an occasional act; one applies to all men and women, the other mostly to farmers and huntsmen. *Yet the Biblical reward is the same for both of these commandments of God!* Long life is promised both for those who honor their parents, and those who are kind to mother birds.

The implications are obvious. God makes no distinction between great virtues and small. He asks that a man be thoughtful and considerate, warm and kindly in every aspect and relationship; that we avoid all evil, great or small, and seek all good for all men.

5

Stand Back and See Life as a Whole

One of the great needs of our time is a sense of perspective. We need to get off and look at life steadily and see it whole.

Max Nordau, the essayist, once suggested a very apt analogy to illustrate the meaning of perspective. Imagine, he suggested, a statue in a public square. Then imagine how that statue looks to an ant crawling on it. We can see at a glance that it is a man mounted on horseback, but an ant could crawl over every single inch of its surface and never know what it was.

So we, like ants, crawl over the surface of current history; we move from headline to headline. We read the daily papers, hear the hourly newscast, but we almost never see the "big picture."

Headlines are like individual whitecaps on the waves. History is like the tide coming in. The daily news is what the human ant sees; a view of history is what he can achieve with perspective.

And surely we need such an overview in these times when history is coming to a climax. It is easy, too easy, with an ant's-eye view to say or do what may provoke a holocaust. It is hard to take the long view, to see the struggle against autocracy and for democracy, against Communism and for freedom, as a long, long struggle that may last for years, even for decades.

To win that struggle will require all the long-range perspective we can muster. Let us, therefore, stand off from the statue and see it as a whole.

But it must be a balanced view, neither through rose-colored glasses nor jaundiced eyes.

Occasionally we meet a real cynic, a man who has nothing good to say of anyone. People are no good; the news is always bad; today's world is worse than yesterday's, and tomorrow will be no better. The real cynic sees no good, hears no good, says no good.

Such men remind me of an old story. In a free-lunch saloon a man once fell asleep over his beer. As he slept, some of his friends smeared Limburger cheese on his mustache. When he awoke, he sniffed the air, made a face, and walked quickly out of the place. He walked down the street and into bar after bar, and every time he sniffed he shuddered. Finally he broke down in tears, and when someone asked what was his trouble, he cried, "The whole world is spoiled!"

Cynicism sometimes grows out of Limburger cheese on the mustache, out of a sour stomach and a bitter soul. Cynics find the bitterness within them reflected in the world about them.

What can we say to cynics? Everything they say is true. But it is not the whole truth.

What we can say is this: "Isn't it a wonderful thing that in a world so full of meanness and selfishness there are instances of nobility and loyalty? Isn't it a remarkable thing that children born with nothing but selfish hungers grow up to be self-sacrificing?" A cynic may be right when he points to the newspaper accounts of knifings, beatings, shootings, but what of the little girl who saved her brother from drowning, what of the sergeant who won the Distinguished Service Cross protecting his company while they retreated from danger; what of the murderer sentenced to the chair who willed his eyes to help the blind? There may be pettiness and hypocrisy all around us, and cruelty and terror. But that's not all. There's kindness, faithfulness to duty, light, and decency.

The beauty of storm clouds

And just as bad as cynicism is faultfinding. At a concert one evening, I overheard a young man saying to his escort, "Did you hear the oboist in that second movement—how he flatted his notes?"

Now I had not heard the oboist flat his notes. Perhaps my ear is not as good as his. But that young man had, and all he had to say about the whole symphony was that the oboe player had made a mistake; all he heard was the flaw. Do you know such people? You ask them how business is, and they cry about how they lost a sale yesterday. Later you discover this was the best year they've ever had, but all they remember is the lost sale. You ask them how they like the beautiful fall weather, and they'll tell you about their hay fever. What sort of young man is their daughter marrying? He drives too fast! How are they feeling? They woke up with a crick in their necks. How do they like the new sanctuary? The brick is the wrong color. All they see is the flaw.

A girl is pretty to look at and bright as a dollar. But her head is turned by her beauty and she becomes very particular. She gets proposals for marriage, but this one is too short (we don't look good when we are dancing), and that one has too many obligations; this one is nice, but not his family; that one does not have enough education. And so down through the years. She just won't let herself fall in love, she sees only the flaw, and suddenly life has passed her by.

A man sits down with the Bible—the beauty of the Twenty-third Psalm, the sweeping grandeur of the Prophets, the ethical vision of Deuteronomy—and what does he see? Only the unanswered questions, where did Cain find his wife? or why does it say in one place that Noah took two of every animal into the ark and in another place that he took seven of each of the clean animals and two of each unclean animal? What does he see in the Bible? Only the flaws.

Why should this be? What gets into us that makes us critical and cynical and bitter, and always ready to find fault, to pick to pieces, to see only the flaw?

Is it to show how smart we are? I suppose the young man was trying to impress his girl when he called attention to the fact that the oboist was flat in the second movement.

Or is it perhaps to be different; is it a way of attracting attention? If everybody says that the Bible is a wonderful book, you can be sure to lift someone's eyebrows if you say it's all bunk.

Or is it because we are unhappy, and when we are unhappy we see only the miserable, the unsightly and flawsome things around us?

Whatever the reason, it is a sad way of life, an unsatisfying way of life. Better by far to look for the good in bad people than for the bad in good folks; better by far to see beauty in the storm clouds than to complain of the rain; better by far to search out and recognize the blessings of life than to curse its flaws. Perhaps the oboist did go flat. Was that all there is to the symphony? Perhaps life does have its sour notes, its bitter tears, its disappointments. Is that all there is? Surely the blessings outweigh by far the curses; surely there is more beauty than ugliness. Surely a cheerful view and an appreciative mind will build a happy heart.

What hope does for man

Above all, perspective requires hope. Every minister has had the experience of trying to arouse hope in the despondent, to give the troubled, the bereaved, the imprisoned a lift of the spirit, a faith in the future. Lift your eyes, we say to the stricken, look up, look ahead; better times are sure to come. Do not let defeat drag you down; do not let sorrow become the quicksand of your life. Hope in the Lord, hope in the Lord.

And every minister will confess to some feeling of helplessness when he is answered, "What good will hope do; what use is there to hope?" How can he explain what hope will do?

He knows what it has done for him, but how can he put it into words that will convince, that will bear the stamp of reason and science as well as of religious faith?

Because I have had this experience of helplessness when people ask what good will hope do, I have been wonderfully inspired by a medical report on hope. In *The Saturday Review of Literature* of January 5, 1957, there was an article by Harold G. Wolff, a professor of medicine at Cornell University Medical College, which he calls "A Scientific Report on What Hope Does for Man." And what Dr. Wolff has to say, and the evidence he brings to prove what he has to say, is so important to all of us that I want to outline it for you.

Dr. Wolff begins by pointing out that life's stresses cause illness and shorten life. Fear, confusion, hopelessness, resignation and failure result in a depressed nervous condition which slows down the health-building processes. Years of life can be pressed out of a man by catastrophe or long duress. Most doctors and ministers have seen sudden death come to people who are overwhelmed with despair. I have seen a man, told that he had about six months to live, just turn his face to the wall and die within a few days.

What makes Dr. Wolff's article interesting, however, are not these statements which concern individuals, but some statistics about the way it works out under scientific observation. If one man loses hope and dies, or another man seizes hope and lives, then this could be taken merely as a coincidence. But if there is a statistical trend, an average covering many people, then we have a scientific fact.

The figures Dr. Wolff has collected concern prisoners of war, both in Europe and in Japan, during the Second World War. Those in Europe were imprisoned on the average about ten months; those in the Pacific about forty months. Likewise, in Japanese prisoner-of-war camps there was far more abuse and humiliation. Six years after liberation, the records of prisoners who had been released were re-examined.

First, they discovered that of those released from Japanese

prisons, three times as many had died as those captured in Europe. And many of these deaths were caused by diseases *not* directly related to confinement or starvation. Heart trouble took twice the number expected, cancer occurred twice as often as normal, and, interestingly, three times as many died in accidents.

What happened to those who survived? It depended largely on how long they had been prisoners of war. The longer their stress and their imprisonment, the more often they were admitted to VA hospitals. And again, their diseases had little to do with what we would expect from such experience. There was a great deal of hernia, deafness, diseases of bones, muscles, and heart.

All of this medical testimony is on the negative side, illustrating the effect of long-deferred hope. But now listen to what Dr. Wolff had to say about the positive side: "A study of a few of the survivors who have since become unusually effective citizens is instructive."

Those who survived the long imprisonment which broke many men were not necessarily those who went into those prisons healthier or stronger. But they were those in whose minds the imprisonment was a painful but only temporary interruption of life. They had hope; they felt as though it would not be long until they would be free. They just knew they would come out alive; they were sure that they would come back home again. And not only did they hope in their hearts, but they found ways of expressing that hope in activity. They focused on the future instead of the present; they looked forward. They made their plans for their vocation, for marriage, family, children, education. They would make lists of the way they were going to spend their time, the kind of food they would eat, and where. It was among these prisoners that courses were organized. They taught each other; they formed tightly knit groups; they believed in each other, helped each other.

In short, prolonged suffering in danger may drain a man

of his health, but on the other hand, he is capable of enduring incredible suffering *if* he has self-respect, hope, purpose, and a belief in his fellows and a belief in God.

This is what our faith has been trying to teach for thousands of years. See life as a whole! Hope. Be not dismayed. Hope thou in the Lord.

6

Pick Your Life's Target

We leave undone so much we intend to do, leave unfinished so much that we start, let drop so much that could be worth while. Most of us live on a hit-or-miss basis. If we would live more effectively and more happily, we need to take closer aim, we need to pick out more carefully our life's target.

There is a story from the Second World War which illustrates this. A long lean mountain boy from Kentucky was called by his draft board back in 1941, and came down out of the mountains to join the Army at Fort Knox. After a few days' training, he was sent out to the rifle range. He had never handled an army rifle, he had never even seen an M-1 before. The mechanism was new to him and somewhat confusing, but as soon as he had learned the knack of operating the weapon, he hung up a new army record for sharpshooting.

The astonished officers asked him how he did it, and he replied, "Well, sir, it's something like this. There are fifteen in my family, and we've always had a hard time scraping together enough to eat. Pop hasn't been able to do much work, and feeding the family has been up to me. Every morning for years, Pop has handed me the old muzzle-loader with a charge of powder and *one* bullet, and he says, 'Here, son, go out and get us some breakfast.' So you see, sir, I haven't been used to doing much missing."

Most of us have been used to doing a lot of missing. We pull the trigger too soon, or wait till too late. We set our sights too high, or we set them too low, or we even aim at the wrong target.

We sometimes shoot too soon.

Young women, made panicky by the marriage of others their age, fearful lest life pass them by, will snatch the first available groom, and then two or three babies later, discover they should have waited for a better target for their love.

A youngster, impatient of the long years of college, has an opportunity for a job that seems to pay well at that moment, takes it, and ends up down a blind alley. He shot too soon, and now, lacking an education, has shot his chances.

And sometimes we shoot too late.

There is a time to be cautious, but there is a time also for adventure. Many a man has missed the target because he waited too long. I can hear a Spanish seaman saying to himself, "Let's just wait and see what happens to this fellow Columbus." The French Army was overrun by the German *Panzers* in 1940 because so few of its generals could see military possibilities in the tank. And imagine what might have been, or might not have been, if Moses had waited for more favorable circumstances to set out on his mission of freedom.

We miss because we aim too low. We fail to lift our sights when important targets are in view, and as a result fail most of our aims.

The good and bad angels

There is an old legend about the Jewish Sabbath which somehow speaks to this failing. As a Jewish worshiper leaves his synagogue at sundown on a Friday evening, two angels accompany him, a good angel and a bad angel. When he arrives home and opens his front door, the angels peek over his shoulder. Now if the house is ready for the Sabbath, if the table is laid with clean linen and shining silver, if the children are well scrubbed and well behaved, and the wife dressed in her Sabbath best with a smile on her face, then the good angel says, "May it be like this all week," and the bad angel has to say a reluctant "Amen." But if, on the other hand, the house is in a turmoil, the Sabbath meal not prepared, the children dirty and quarreling, the wife in a shrewish mood, then the bad angel says with malicious glee, "May it be like this all week," and the good angel must say a sad "Amen."

When I was a youngster and would hear this story from my rabbi's lips, I used to wonder why it was that the other angel was required to say Amen. Why, if the bad angel said, "Let it be like this," the good angel couldn't say, "Oh no, it does not have to be." Only the years and experience have taught that it isn't the angels who bless or curse, but the laws of life themselves. If, at life's loveliest moments, we fail to measure up, then we can expect the average moments to lack any beauty at all. If, when joy of spirit and high emotions are called for, we fall down, then how low our lives will sink in the routine round. Only if the Sabbath is truly a Sabbath can the weekdays partake of glory. But if the Sabbath is a week-day, then what will the weekdays be like?

If a couple quarrel on their honeymoon, how much happiness can they expect when the honeymoon is over? If a boy forgets his mother on Mother's Day, how much can she expect from him on the other three hundred and sixty-four days of the year?

If a man simply cannot give up his golf game while one of the children is sick, what sort of father will he be when they are well? This is the implication of the legend of the Sabbath angels, when in life's high moments we act in low fashion, then the level of our living sinks to new lows.

This is why, it seems to me, we have always tried to surround our important occasions with so much of pomp and ceremony, of beauty and loveliness—to lift them above the ordinary days and through them to transform the ordinary days. Birthdays are not necessary to life except to record one's age, yet most of us celebrate, and on them give and receive gifts, light candles and blow them out. And for the simplest reason; to rejoice in the gift of life, in the advancing

years, and to lift the heart above the routine of day that follows day. Married couples are not required to have anniver-
sary celebrations, but they do, to remind them of the day of
days when their love was blessed, to recall together the years
of sweet companionship, to express again the high hopes and
dreams with which they set out on the marital seas—in short,
to give to the routine of marriage a lift and a soaring spirit.

This is why all of us who love our religion want our houses
of worship to be beautiful, our services of prayer to be well
planned, our music to be inspiring. It is because after the
week of toil and before another week of the same toil, we
want a few moments of high inspiration in a place that radi-
ates with quiet beauty; we want our moments with God to be
a little finer, a little higher, a little more solemn than the ev-
eryday moments. We don't want slang in our prayers, nor
popular ditties in our choir lofts. We want to be lifted. We
want to hear the good angel say, "May it be like this all
week."

So it is if we lift our sights when the great targets are in
view; we shall be able to achieve our goals in the humdrum of
every day. Let the good angel help us aim, and the bad angel
will have to say, "Bull's-eye!"

But there is also a danger in aiming too high, in setting
one's sights on targets that are out of our range.

The boat in the basement

Some years ago, a man in Michigan built a boat in his basement. The boat was eight feet wide, the basement door was
only three feet wide and six feet tall. I don't know what he
decided to do—whether to knock out an opening in his basement wall or take his boat apart. His story made the papers
all over the country. You would think, wouldn't you, that people would learn? It's happened so often, and we've read about
so many, surely none of us would make so foolish a mistake.
But it happened again this past week near my hometown.

And it's been happening, I suppose, as long as men have

been making things. I recall mention of a man who lived more than a hundred years ago. A clever Yankee invented a safety match, and New England rather than Sweden might have been the center of the match industry, if it hadn't been for this man's miscalculation. He went to build a factory to manufacture safety matches, and when it came to providing water power, he built a water wheel too big for the amount of water in the stream by which he built his factory. He became so discouraged he dropped the whole thing.

And, of course, a story like this suggests a great many life-situations that we see around us every day. How many of us have built water wheels too big for the stream to turn, nursed ambitions too big for our abilities, and then because we have planned too large, become discouraged and given up the whole project.

People who are overweight have sometimes hurt themselves seriously by trying to take off too much at once, and others, because the ounces came off so slowly, and the chocolate cake looked so good, get on and off diets as often as they get on and off scales.

Boys go to college, start out in a professional course of study, find it difficult, switch to another line of study, find it harder too than they are willing to work, and finally drop college altogether.

The doctor tells us we need exercise—we get all of our equipment together, we huff and we puff until we are worn out. The next day we can't even move, and the doctor's suggestions are forgotten.

This is also true in the spiritual qualities. We so often bite off more than we can chew, set our goal at one hundred per cent, dream of perfection. We build a water wheel of dreams too large for the stream of will power.

So often, in life's solemn hours, we pledge ourselves to complete revolutions of attitude and behavior, and then, failing in one or another aspect of character, give ourselves up as hopeless. In the development of our souls, we need to set ourselves realizable goals, goals not only to which we can aspire but which we also can attain.

Picking life's targets requires cautious judgment on the one hand and adventurous daring on the other. It demands that we aim toward the highest goals of which we are capable, but not at targets beyond our range. Like the young mountaineer, we have to learn that no matter how much game there may be, we've only one bullet to shoot, one life to live, and we must therefore "get used to not missing."

7

Accept Your Role in Life

To live with ourselves, we must accept ourselves as we are and can be, without regrets for what we are not or cannot be. We need to build the water wheel the right size. Some might call this facing bitter reality, but others would call it wisdom.

That wisdom calls for honest and humble self-judgment, a willingness to strive, and a satisfaction in whatever we achieve.

The general principles are expressed in an old rabbinic story.

There was once a very wise teacher who used to give his pupils as a graduation present a little two-pocket purse, and in each pocket a slip of paper with a sentence on it. In one pocket of the purse was the sentence: "For my sake was the world created." In the other pocket were the words: "I am but dust and ashes."

Oh, the paradox of human life! We are children of God and, at the same time, children of earth. We are the crown of creation, and yet but dust and ashes.

"For my sake was the world created." We need this. When we fritter away our time on vanity, when we work to eat and eat to work like a beast of burden, or when, like a butterfly, we live for a good time, we ought to reach into that pocket and read: "For my sake was the world created."

Or when life loses its meaning and nobility, when we begin to say, "What's the difference? We'll all be dead in a hundred years," then it is time to seek a renewed sense of life's importance. "For my sake was the world created."

On the other hand, "I am but dust and ashes." When we get to feeling smug and proud, when we begin to think the whole world is our oyster, then we need to remember it.

Or, if we become absorbed in wealth, we need to remember that there are no pockets in shrouds. "We are but dust and ashes."

It all adds up to this: We need pride in ourselves, but a pride tempered by humility.

The essence of true humility

Humility is a rare quality, and even more rarely understood. Humility has usually been associated with a shy and retiring manner, with the avoidance of any show, with a quiet stay-in-the-corner personality. This is the very opposite of our present-day successful personality-image, which is aggressive, expansive, and in the middle of things.

Unfortunately we mistake the outer pattern of behavior for the inner attitude, and therefore humility is quite neglected in today's vocabulary. An old story out of Jewish lore will illustrate the problem. A king was once told that humility would lengthen life, and wanting to live to a ripe old age, he tried to humble himself. He moved from his great palace to a little hut, he put aside his regal robes and dressed in homespun, he forbade anyone to bow to him or pay him extravagant compliments. He was going to be humble, and everybody was going to know it.

But his adviser, a wise and warmhearted rabbi, said to him, "My lord, you have mistaken the essence of humility. You *are* a king, so dress like a king, live like a king, allow people to show you the respect due a king, but be humble in your inmost heart."

The meaning is clear. Humility is not a manner, humility is a quality. The humble man does not refuse to listen to compliments; he just does not take them too seriously. The humble man does not deny himself the appropriate symbols of his achievement, but he does not attach any importance to them. The humble man remembers that he is the creature and not the Creator, that good fortune plays a great role in life, that if he stands tall, it is because he is standing on the shoulders of those who have gone before him. He is humble in his heart.

Humility can, of course, be overdone.

Rabbi Zussya came into a sickroom one day to find a member of his congregation in tears. Putting his hand sympathetically upon the patient's shoulder, the rabbi asked, "Mendel, why do you cry? My dear friend, what troubles you?"

"Oh, Rabbi," the sick man sobbed, "I have been reading my Bible about Moses, what a wonderful man he was, what a fine character he had, and what great things he achieved. And it has made me feel so unworthy, so insignificant. If it is God's will that I die of this illness, what shall I say when I face my Maker? How can I find favor in His sight, when in comparison to Moses, I am so unworthy?"

Zussya smiled. "Mendel," he said, "God will not ask you why you weren't Moses; God will only ask why you weren't Mendel."

God does not demand of us what is impossible for us. He does not expect of us more than we are capable of. He does not expect a pine tree to bear apples, or a live oak to put forth roses. We need not feel unworthy by comparison to a Moses, an Einstein, a Salk, or a Schweitzer. To these men much was given, and from them much is expected. We are not unworthy because we have not achieved what they have.

But on the other hand, God does demand of us what *is* possible. He insists that we live by the best in us. He does not expect peaches from a carrot seed, but He does expect a good carrot! He does not ask, "Why weren't you Moses?"

Unless, of course, you are Moses.

At first, Moses beat around the burning bush. He did not want to be Moses the Emancipator. He was afraid of the challenge to greatness. He squirmed with excuses before he accepted his call.

Moses had finally found peace of mind. The terrible sight of his brothers in Egypt slaving away their lives had faded from his memory. True, he had tried to help them; he had actually killed a cruel taskmaster as he was about to whip a Hebrew slave, but they did not appreciate it. They did not want him or his favors, and they informed on him, so that Pharaoh knew that this young man, whom the princess had rescued and raised, was a rebel, a revolutionary, and a dangerous character. The police were sent for but Moses eluded them and went into exile, probably with a price on his head.

In the wilderness, Moses met and married a beautiful girl, whose father was a head man in those parts; he had children to dandle on his knee, and a secure future as the son-in-law of a wealthy man. And then God called. Out of the burning bush he said, "Come now, therefore, and I will send thee to Pharaoh that thou mayest bring forth My people, the children of Israel out of Egypt."

And Moses beat around the bush. "Who am I," he said, "that I should go to Pharaoh, and that I should bring forth the children of Israel out of Egypt?" Then God said, "You will not be alone. I will go with you." And Moses found another excuse, "When they ask in whose name I speak, what will I say?"

Then God told Moses His name, and went into detail about how Moses was to gather the elders and speak to Pharaoh and instruct the people. But Moses still hung back. "Surely, I will tell them God sent me, and then they will say, 'How do we know God sent you? God has not appeared to you.'"

God answered this objection too, but Moses still did not want to go. "God," he said, "I can't talk. I am a stammerer and a stutterer." Again God was patient. "I'll put the words in your mouth, Moses," He said.

And then Moses quit beating around the burning bush, and came right out and suggested that God send someone else—

Aaron or anyone He wished, but not him. Then God lost patience and became angry, and Moses went down to Egypt.

It wasn't easy, friends. He did not want to go, but he had to.

Most of us have it a little easier. We manage to stifle the voice of conscience and evade its call. We beat around the bush until it burns out, don't we? The call comes to every man to do what he can do to right the wrongs of this world. We see dishonesty around us, we know of corruption in high places, we see the abuse of people, and the destruction of fine institutions; we see slavery of the mind which is ignorance, and slavery of the spirit which is the fear of power, and we feel the call. We hear God's voice as clearly as did Moses that day on the western slope of Sinai, and we beat around the bush.

Who am I, we say, a nobody, a simple citizen without any ability at all—no, I can't go. And then our conscience says, "Man alone is nobody. Man with God is everybody." But we still resist. "Who will believe that I am obeying God? They will just say I am out for some selfish gain, out to feather my own nest. They won't believe me." And again the voice will sound, and again we will find an excuse, until the inner fire dies and our conscience leaves us at rest, and a little bit of the Godliness within us shrivels and dies away.

If there is within us the potentials of a Moses, then one day the question will be asked, "Why weren't you like Moses?"

The badge of your work

The only way we will ever know whether we were supposed to be like Moses or not will be by putting forth the effort. There are very few great men; but without great effort there will be none. The fourth commandment bids us to rest on the Sabbath but it also bids us to work on the weekdays. Too many of us regard work as something to avoid; the harder the work, the more desirable the avoidance. But inherently in the scheme of things labor has dignity, all labor whether of hand or of head.

So often people think of work as one of the curses God laid on Adam and his descendants, "in the sweat of thy brow," etc., but rabbinic interpretation of the Genesis story suggests just the opposite.

When Adam and Eve were driven from the Garden of Eden, God's first statement was this: "Thorns and thistles shall it bring forth to you, and you shall eat the herb of the field." Upon hearing this, according to legend, Adam cried aloud in complaint to God: "What? Am I to crop grass like a horse or a cow? Am I to be no different from my animals?"

God heard Adam's plea and changed His mind: "In the sweat of your brow shall you eat your bread." And Adam was content; he had been given the gift of work; he felt dignified by labor.

Labor does dignify man. It reflects his higher nature. Though many a housewife looks enviously at domestic animals who cook not, neither do they wash dishes; though many a man wishes he could live like the wild horse who makes no payments on house or car, the fact is that man's progress, man's achievements, man's civilization are built upon the sweat of his brow. Whether he works with his hands or his head, whether he fashions ideas or things, his labor is dignified. "Every man is proud of his profession," said one Talmudic sage, "for he shows off the badge of his work. The butcher wears his apron around his waist, the driver carries a whip, the shepherd a staff, the scribe walks about with his pen behind his ear." All work has dignity, and every workman can walk with pride in his labor.

White-collar workers sometimes think themselves superior to men who must work with their hands; laborers, on the other hand, were taught by Marx to despise the middleman. Thus, in so many ways, men are vocational snobs and tend to look down their noses at the way others earn their living.

Yet our whole world is built on a division of labor, and every way of work is vitally important to the whole. As long as a man does what comes to his hand to do, and does it honestly and with diligence, he is contributing to the sum total of human welfare. Without cotton pickers, none of us would have a shirt to his back, but with cotton pickers alone, we would have cotton and no cloth. Without factory workers in New Orleans, wholesale houses in Dallas, stores in Houston, the cotton would never get from the warehouse to our possession. Railroad men have to handle the freight, truckers to get it to the retail outlet, and a businessman has to pay the freight bill before anything is available for us. The food we eat, the clothes we wear are the products of thousands of skills and millions of hands. The thinker, the teacher, the banker, the inventor, the engineer, the designer, the weaver, the electrician—every single one of them are vital, and if one of them fails in his task, then all of us are the poorer. So, too, each of us is important, no matter what our work or profession, to the welfare of all others. All men need all others.

The rabbis of the Talmud knew this well. Tempted to intellectual snobbery by their learning and the honor paid them, they repeated these words to themselves:

"I am a creature of God, my neighbor is also His creature.

"My work is in the city, his is in the field.

"I rise early to do my work, he rises early to his.

"As he cannot excel in my work, so I cannot do well in his.

"But perhaps you say, I do great things and he does small things. We are taught that it does not matter whether a man works at great tasks or little, as long as he directs his heart to Heaven."

You don't have to be a genius

All work is hard, and no amount of ability can replace diligent labor. The Nobel prize-winning physicist Ernest Orlando Lawrence said, "You don't have to have genius to be a scientist—just character. All you have to do is work hard and figure things out."

But this sort of statement is not restricted to scientists. It applies to music: Paderewski used to say, "Before I was a genius, I was a drudge." It applies to literature: Editor Alfred Funk said, "I have never discovered a genius who spoke of talent or even inspiration. Only brutal work."

It looks as though they all agree. Work, hard work, drudgery if you will, is the ultimate key to achievement. Granted you have to have some intelligence, some ability, some skill, it still takes work and more of it.

We do not like to face this fact. We like to think of a composer sitting under a blossom-laden appletree dreaming up a spring song, writing a few notes on paper and presto! there it is. We like to think of an architect dreaming of new forms, a designer making a few pencil strokes, an artist casually putting his brush to paper, a minister suddenly moved to preach a sermon.

But that is not the way it is. Sometimes inspiration comes like a flash, sometimes we have to wrack our brains, but whether the original thought comes fast or slow, there is still work to do, the work of harmonizing, the work of plans and specifications, the work of filling in the pencil strokes, the work of finishing the picture, the work of organizing and writing the story or sermon. And that work is hard work, and let no one tell you differently. Before anyone can be a genius, he must be a drudge.

But please remember I did not promise you that if you are a drudge, then you will be sure to be a genius. I wish it were so, but it is not. However, even drudges can and should take comfort in the fact that their drudgery can help bring out genius.

Once I joined other parents at a dance studio to watch our young daughters demonstrate their achievements. As I watched the little girls go through their still limited ballet exercises, I learned a lesson for life.

The youngsters were typical of their age. Some were thin, some were not; some were more graceful and some less; but all of them were quite serious, all of them were trying. Suddenly, beyond and behind them I felt as though I could see a leading ballerina. You have seen how, in motion pictures, they sometimes impose a shadowy form over the picture. This is what it was like—the ghostly larger-than-life form of the great Margot Fonteyn performing with perfect grace of body, arms, and hands the same steps and gestures that these little girls were striving at so hard.

In that moment I realized that greatness is built not only upon individual skill but also upon group efforts. Human achievements are rather like a pyramid. A pyramid is so constructed that its height depends entirely upon its base; the only way the top can go higher is to make the base larger. The Pavlovas and Margot Fonteyns in the world of ballet are built upon the thousands of little girls whose mothers dutifully drive them to class and whose fathers dutifully come to see their progress. Not all of them will be great, but they provide the incentive for teachers and for studios which form the base for the pyramid.

So it is with all of life. This is what we are trying to do with our current emphasis on science education. Not every youngster who now takes it up will be an Einstein, but the more our boys and girls are exposed to such studies, the more possibilities there are of an Einstein at the top.

This is what happened in the Bible. Elijah was left alone, and so he produced little that is permanent. But Isaiah and Jeremiah, preceded by great men like Elijah, surrounded by prophetic schools, rose to greater heights and left us an inspired literature.

This all points to the part that each of us can play in life— to attach ourselves to great causes, to seek great truths, to become building stones in pyramids that can rise only as high as we build them.

Little girls taking ballet lessons make Pavlovas possible.

Little people living great lives help bring God's Kingdom. And let's not leave out the boys.

The scrub team is the team to watch

All of us who are interested in football know the names of the players on our local teams, whether high school or college. Most of us know the names of the outstanding football players on other teams in our conference and all over the nation. But there are a great number of football players whose names we do not know, and probably never will. Yet they are as great as football heroes, and perhaps even greater than those who made the All-American. In fact, without them, we would probably not have any football worth watching. The football players I refer to are the members of the scrub team, the boys who never quite make the first and second teams, but who go out on the practice field afternoon after afternoon, and work just as hard as any player who gets his letter. They get no glory, they get no cheers; they get only hard work. The scrub team gets worked on. They get out on the field against the first team, they get tackled and blocked and knocked over. Why? So the first team can be strong. They do all that hard grinding work so that the first team can go out and win their games on the week end. Before a big game, the scrub team learns the plays of the visiting team and tries them out on the first team for practice. Without the scrubs, the first teams would never be what they are. It is, therefore, the scrubs, the unsung heroes that I would praise.

And, as a colleague of mine has pointed out, you will find them everywhere, doing the work that needs doing, carrying the jobs that must be carried, getting little or none of the glory, and yet getting so much of satisfaction.

David Lilienthal, the chairman of the Atomic Energy Commission, tells a story in his book, *This I Do Believe,* about a woman whose job at Oak Ridge atomic plant had been to run a vacuum over the floor of the great plant where atom bombs were being made. She had never been told what they were manufacturing; all she did was run a vacuum cleaner. When the bomb was dropped, and the folks at Oak Ridge realized what they had been working on, someone asked her what she had done to help build the bomb. "I was sweeping up them atom husks," she replied, with a great deal of pride. She was a member of the scrub team, yet without her, dust might have accumulated and ruined the experiments.

In the old days when organs had to be pumped by hand, a great organist gave a beautiful recital and was well applauded. The boy who pumped the organ said, "We gave a fine concert, didn't we?"

The scrub team is the team to watch. Let the scrub team begin to fail and the first team will show it. Let the organ pumper stop his pumping and there will be no music.

The scrub team is the team that most of us are on. In this great democracy of ours, there are very few solo parts. No one of us carries the fate of the nation in his hands, but in all of our hands together is the destiny of our nation and of all nations. It is then by each of us doing his task, in integrity and in pride in the part he plays, that the great work gets done, and if we on the scrub team do our part, God's first team will win the game of humanity.

The little cake-baking jobs

A noted orator once stirred an audience with his picture of the world's ills and the way to heal them. He called for every ounce of effort his listeners could muster for the solution of mankind's problems. He pleaded for an heroic response to the great challenge of the times. When he finished his magnificent oration, a little old lady came up to shake his hand and said, "I am not sure I understand everything you want us to do, but could I maybe bake a cake?"

I used to laugh at that story, but during the war I came to realize how profound it is.

It happened in the Philippines. Our Sixth Division was

fighting its way across the central mountain range of Luzon, east of Manila. Most of the headquarters and aid stations were in hillside caves. It was outside one such aid station that we held worship services one noon. The men had come in from the company headquarters and the battlefield itself, not in "go-to-meeting" clothes, but in battle dress. After the prayer service was over, some of the men sat around for a few minutes waiting for transportation back to their outfits and I happened to overhear a conversation between two GIs. They were both company cooks, and *they were exchanging recipes for white cake!* One of them said to the other, "I always put frosting on my cakes. I don't care how much trouble it takes, if my buddies are out there getting shot at, the least I can do is give them a good meal."

I have never forgotten that conversation. It was a real lesson for life. The great tasks of humankind, the gigantic problems we face, mostly break down into little cake-baking jobs.

Perhaps the pilot has the glamour, but without mechanics he cannot get off the ground. Perhaps the machine gunner seems to make a bigger noise, but someone has to cook his food.

And not only in war, but the homes in which we live, the governments which protect us, the world peace we seek are ultimately the result of little people volunteering to bake a cake, or, to change the figure, make a sacrifice hit.

Once I tried to explain to our daughter what a sacrifice hit is. And while I was explaining this familiar baseball practice, whereby a batter deliberately sacrifices himself to advance a runner from first to second base, I suddenly realized how well the term describes the lives of many noble men and women whom I know.

I think of a man who went to work so that his brilliant young brother could have a college education. I think of parents who gave up all luxuries and took no vacation for years so that their talented child could have the best musical education money could buy. I think of runners who never win a race, but by pacing champions, help break world records. I think of Jonathan who stepped aside so that another man, his friend David, might ascend the throne of a kingdom.

Sacrifice hits: What of the hero who exposed himself to yellow fever that others might advance a base in health? What of teachers who might earn greater incomes in industry, but who love to teach and to help unfold the minds of youngsters? What of the soldier who put his foot on a grenade to save the lives of his buddies?

It is not always easy. A fellow wants to swing his bat and try for a home run. It's not easy to efface yourself, to put yourself out of the running to help another advance a base, to help a team win a game. It's not easy, but it's the mark of a good baseball player, and it's the mark of a good man in the game of life. Therefore, when God signals us to make a sacrifice hit, let us follow His command.

"Isaac Abrahams made a motion . . ."

As a chaplain of the American Legion, I was invited to take part in ceremonies at the Tomb of the Unknown Soldier. These meditations came to my mind, and in my heart I said to those buried there:

"Here in the midst of the known you lie unknown; yet someday the known will be forgotten and you will be remembered.

"They who lie beneath gravestones that bear their names are visited now by those who loved them. But for how long? Those who remember them will one day travel the same road —their ranks are thinned each year—until the day comes when all who remember are themselves but memories, and the monument of each known becomes unknown.

"But the Unknowns? To their tomb men will come year after year, decade after decade, century after century, and through remembering them, will recall all those who lie around them who died that liberty might live."

And isn't this the story of mankind's long life? Who is remembered from ages past? From the days of the Exodus, only a Moses, an Aaron, a Miriam. And who followed Moses through the parted sea? The unknown. Who saw the cloud rest on Sinai? The unknown. Those who buried them loved them; to them they were known, but to us no name is left. And yet, what would history have been without them? Had none of those unknowns, those nameless little people, followed Moses, he, too, would be unknown.

You and I may leave no visible monument in this world, at least for long. We shall die and crumble to dust and above our graves the tombstones will be wet with the tears of those who remember until they, too, shall lie down in death.

Yet, unknown, we, too, shall live. If we believe in liberty, struggle for justice, seek peace, then we shall live in the achievements of mankind alongside those of our time whose names shall be known to all ages.

This same thought came to me on another occasion when I was browsing over some books and manuscripts in the archives of the Hebrew Union College-Jewish Institute of Religion in Cincinnati. I came upon the Minutes Book of one of the oldest congregations in America, and therein I read a sentence which has stayed with me: "Isaac Abrahams made a motion . . ."

I have forgotten what the motion was. It may have been to build a new fence around the cemetery, or to change the Everlasting Light from oil to gas, but all I remember is that Isaac Abrahams made a motion.

Nor is it too clear who Isaac Abrahams was. Obviously he was a member of the congregation who had come to the annual meeting, but was he a member of the board? Was he important or obscure, rich or poor, old or young, married or single, successful or a failure? This it did not say; all it said was that Isaac Abrahams made a motion.

And somehow I cannot get out of my mind the thought

that little sentence aroused in me—that history is actually made up of all the Isaac Abrahams who make motions.

There was a meeting one night in Boston, Massachusetts. A group of young and ardent men gathered to talk over the newest indignity by George III. There was taxation without representation flung into the very teeth of the colonists. Someone that night made a motion, and the United States was born.

There must have been a meeting one night in Egypt when Aaron brought his brother Moses to talk with a group of Hebrew elders about a vast new dream he had. Who knows how long they discussed, debated it, worried about it, but then someone must have made a motion, and the Exodus began to take shape.

Somehow at every turning point in history, there is someone who brings the discussion into focus, who turns the discontent into constructive channels, who holds up the standard to which men can repair, who says, "I make a motion." The world has been moved by the motions of the Isaac Abrahams, the little people, scrub team members, cake bakers, drudges, Unknown Soldiers.

Mr. Abrahams, you have the floor. What is your motion?

8

Living with Courage

There is a story I have mulled over many times. A little girl was groping her way near the docks through a dense fog. Feeling alone and lost, she began to cry with fright. Suddenly she heard a man's voice calling her, "This way, little girl," and guided by his words, she made her way to an open door and the snug safety of a human dwelling. A venerable old man made her at home before the fire, and as her sobbing quieted, he said, "Now, you know faith. When God says, 'Go into the fog,' you go." Out of her tears the little one replied, "But I don't like the fog." The old man's eyes were somber, "We don't have to like it."

We don't have to like it—did you hear those words? Do they haunt your soul as they do mine? We do not have to like it. God sends us out into the fog, out into the unknown, out into the mission that takes all the courage we have, but He does not tell us we have to like it.

We usually think of courage as gay, as something insouciant and debonair. We think of heroes as swashbucklers almost swaggering through danger. And then we look within ourselves and see all the craven fears and timidity, and we say, "I can't be a hero. I'm afraid; I don't like the fog." We don't have to like it.

When we recall the heroism of the Maccabees, the struggle for religious liberty which physically and spiritually kept Judaism alive, we do well to think again of those words. For as I read the story of the Maccabees in the Apocrypha, I find the story of many an heroic act, but never any empty boasting, never any fearless swagger—they did it without liking it. It would have been wonderful, I suppose, if the Maccabees had felt like Robin Hood in all the stories we read and the movies we see. What fun it seems. Living out in the open under the stars, laughing at the forces of the enemy, having a gay old time as an outlaw. But that is not the way it was. It was grimy and dirty; in the summer it was hot and dry; in the winter, cold and wet. No roof over their heads, no tenderness, no children's voices, nothing but the fog of an interminable war and the rustle of the enemy's scouts all about. They did it, but they did not have to like it.

Life calls us, God calls us, constantly to stand up and be counted, to take up a burden, to shoulder a pack, to support a cause, to do a job. It sends us out into the wilderness of illness, it demands that we walk through the valley of the shadow, it imposes obligations heavier than we can bear. But we do not have to like it.

Too often the religious life is presented as one of almost gaiety—as though God's every burden becomes a light burden, and every fog easy to see through. Some of the ideas I read, and some of the talks I hear treat life and its foggy problems as though with just a little prayer and a little faith, the fog would lift. But suppose it does not! It does not have to be easy, and we do not have to like it.

It is no trick at all to be a hero while the newspapers are crying you up, when those who know you shout huzza, when you lead the parade. The hero is the man who does not like it, but does it anyway.

Think of the women who have been the breadwinners while their husbands have been sick. Think of the girls who kept the homes fires burning while their soldier men were away. Think of the men who spent months in a submarine, or others pursuing some distant vision in a laboratory. Think of those who kept at jobs they did not like because little mouths must be fed. You don't have to like it. You only have to do it.

Courage not only demands the unpleasant; courage is often lonely, standing against the opinion of the world.

And it is such courage of which the world has need in every age.

Last week I made a visit to a prison. And while I was there a young man told me of how he got there. It was an old, old story. He had run with the wrong company. He got in with the wrong crowd. They began with little things, smoking, drinking, gambling, and then moved on to more. The time came when the gang's leader suggested robbing a liquor store. This young man objected a little. And their answer to him was, "What's the matter, are you afraid?" And so to show them that he was not afraid, he went along. But you see he really was afraid—he was afraid of their opinion. He could not hold out against the crowd. The courage he lacked was the courage to stand alone, to say, "Even if all of you have decided that this is the right thing to do, I will not do it."

Where would our world be without men who stood alone? Abraham of old stood up and defied all the people of his time, and said, "You're wrong—these are not gods, nor these, nor these. God cannot be seen, God cannot be touched. God is spirit, God is one."

And so it was with an Amos who refused to be silenced by the majority of his day, or Jeremiah who denounced the popular prophets who cried, "Peace, peace," when there was no peace. Oh you know their names, they are written in the books of man—scientists and religionists, doctors and engineers, statesmen and humble citizens—men and women who have had the courage to stand alone until they won the world to their viewpoint. Without them, we'd still be living in caves and carrying clubs, still bowing down to idols. The world has been pushed forward by men who stood alone.

The hired boy and the duke

This same quality of courage is revealed in a story I once read. The Duke of Wellington, known as the man of iron will, the general who stood up to Napoleon and defeated him at Waterloo, loved to ride through the English countryside in the sport of fox hunting. Now the huntsmen on their horses were not too considerate of property, and it was a constant complaint of the farmers during the hunting season that the horses trampled their crops and ruined their gardens. So one English farmer sent his hired boy, when he knew a fox hunt was in the neighborhood, to guard the front gate and not allow huntsmen to pass. A group of men in red coats on big horses thundered up to the gate and their leader, a man of dignified and noble bearing, ordered the boy to open the gate. The boy refused. Whereupon the horseman said, "Boy, do you know who I am? I am the Duke of Wellington and I am not accustomed to disobedience. I command you to open this gate." The boy took off his cap in respect, but said in a firm voice, "I am sure the Duke of Wellington would not wish me to disobey the orders of my employer."

The Duke sat on his horse for a moment in complete silence, then looking steadfastly at the lad, lifted his hat and said, "I honor the man or the boy who is faithful to his duty, and who cannot be frightened into doing wrong."

That is the sort of story that makes the heart sing, because we identify ourselves with that boy who held his ground against the biggest man in England. That's the sort of person we wish we were, independent, fearless, strong. And yet in our own lives how often we truckle to the powerful of the world. How often we yield to the pressure of public opinion. How often we keep our mouths from speaking the truth, and close our eyes to the evils of society.

And it is this very fear which so often creates the evils of this world. What is it that makes a child a bully? It may begin with something inside him, but it grows on the fact that others allow themselves to be bullied by him. What is it that sometimes makes "little Caesars" out of men with authority? Not their authority, but the fear of those under them. Men who are rich are sometimes little dictators. Why? Because men praise them, fawn upon them, fall all over themselves to do their bidding. But let any man stand up and say, "I do not care who you are, what you have, or who put you in your job; I do not fear you and I will not obey you," and the balloon of the bully is burst.

It has been the brave men through the ages, who have stood fearlessly against all power and might, who have done most to redeem human life. David against Goliath, the Minute Men of Concord against the majesty of the King of England, these have been the men who, like the lad who stood up to Wellington, knew the meaning of courage.

Courage is doing what we do not enjoy doing; courage is being willing to stand alone; courage is being first to undertake the unpleasant task.

When I was in high school, football was a much rougher game than it is today. Today, once the ball carrier's knee has touched the ground he's down, and the play is over. But in the old days the ball carrier might fall or be thrown several times during a play. He had to be down and held down before the play was over. The result was that at the end of every scrimmage, there were usually ten or eleven men piled up on top of the ball carrier and the tackler. The boys used to get hurt frequently that way. I suppose that's why they changed the rule.

Now during those days, it is recalled, some coaches were discussing a well-known football player and asking each other whether he was really as good as the sports writers seemed to think. There was a referee in the group, and one of the coaches turned to him and said, "You've seen him play. What do you think?" The referee answered, "Well, I'm not sure but what he was a great passer and kicker, but when it came to tackling—well, I never had to dig him out from the bottom of a scrimmage." Do you follow his thought? That boy was never the first one to do the tackling; he was always one of the gang that would run and jump on top of the pile after someone else had got him down, and then after the scrimmage was over, would say, "We sure stopped them that time, didn't we?"

It is not only in football games that we meet such characters; there are many folks who wait for someone else to do the tackling, and then pile on and act as though they had done the job.

Going over to help your buddies

You can sit and listen to someone talking about political corruption or bad business practices of which he heartily disapproves. Then you say to him, "Why don't we do something about this?" And he will answer, "Oh no, not me, I am too little a fellow to tackle such a big problem. Why should I stick my neck out? They would just run over me like a steam roller." But let someone else, someone no bigger than he, make the first tackle, then our friend comes running up to jump on the top of the scrimmage.

Back in the twenties when the Klan was in full cry, there were only a few brave souls who went out to make the tackle. But once the Klan began to slip, then a lot of the people who had disapproved loudly in private, but publicly kept very quiet, ran and jumped on the pile and talked about how *we* stopped the Klan.

I recall a time in New Guinea when one of our battalions had been ambushed and was being cut to pieces, and another battalion in the same regiment was ordered to their rescue. The boys began to grumble about suicide missions, and some of the officers showed a remarkable lack of interest. Suddenly the battalion chaplain started off toward the distant sound of guns. "I don't know about you fellows," he said very casually but in a voice that carried, "but I am going over there to help our buddies." And immediately the whole battalion joined him, and oh, how they talked the next day about how *we* beat the Japs. The chaplain, however, was at the bottom of the scrimmage.

When you stop to think about it, all of our religious heroes are men who could be found at the bottom of the scrimmage, always the first to tackle, the first to get in there against overwhelming opposition. And after they had made the tackle, then people joined them, then people followed them. But all of us who call ourselves players on God's great team, ought always to be found at the bottom of the scrimmage.

9

Living with Problems

One of my most vivid memories is of a Halloween when our children were still tiny. They could not be allowed out after dark alone. And so, when dusk came on, when they put on their costumes and their masks and went out to join the other children in the neighborhood in "trick or treat," I went with them. I did not hold their hands or even stay right beside them, but just walked along the street while they went from door to door, their little voices shrilling at each door, "Trick or treat."

In the shadows of night, lit only by the early stars and electric street lights, there was something magically beautiful about the whole scene. The children did not seem to have any feet, they scudded across the grass like leaves blown by the wind; their happy voices had a lilt that only the most beautiful music can recapture; and the doorways lit up in answer to their calls with the welcome warm beams of light that betokened the wonderful hospitality of neighbors. Their sacks were soon loaded with fruit and candy and all sorts of goodies as they went from door to door calling, "Trick or treat."

And I wondered, as I walked and watched, what they would do if there were no treat. They were too young to know what a trick is, they only knew that on this magic night the door would open and a kind hand would place in theirs something sweet, something tasty, something good.

And I could not help thinking that night, and I cannot help thinking now as I recall its haunting quality, that our lives are something like that. We run from door to door as long as we live, and wait for the doors to open, wondering, "Will it be trick or treat?"

We knock on the door of the doctor's office; we knock on the door that has a sign, MAN WANTED; we knock on the door of the one we love with a ring in our pocket. All our lives, we knock on doors, hoping and praying that it will be treat and not trick.

A young man knocks on the door of a career, a job, a calling, a vocation. What will it be, trick or treat? Will he find happiness in a work in which he feels useful, or misery in a drudgery that has neither meaning nor satisfaction. Many have chosen a life work only to find it without challenge. How many of us have the courage to go out and begin to knock on new doors, to find a way of earning a living which produces satisfaction as well as income?

We knock on the door of marriage, and love lets us in. We anticipate, we hope, we dream of the long years together. What will it be? Trick or treat, lack of understanding, quarreling, separation; or growing sympathy, deepening understanding, widening love?

Parents knock on the hospital door, the maternity ward entrance, and new life comes into the home. Will it be trick or treat? Will it grow to be a source of pride, of joy, or of shame and despair?

Our children are too young to understand—we know. We know that the doors of life do not all fly open to our knock, do not all yield us sweetmeats and goodies; behind many a door there stand disappointment, tragedy, grief. Yet we go on knocking on those doors, forever hoping that life will be more treat than trick; that somehow when the books are all balanced, they who walk uprightly and try to do justly will discover that the game was worth the candle. For them all the tricks of life will not snuff out their childlike capacity for joy and their faith that, though every door of life be slammed in their face, behind the last door of all there will stand their Maker and their Friend, that He will not trick, that with Him is the treat of redemption now and forever.

Don't get absorbed by petty irritations

In learning to handle the tricks life plays on us we need a perspective. We can get it from the suggestion made by the psychiatrist, Dr. Viktor Frankl, in his book, *From Death Camp to Existentialism*. Dr. Frankl points out that just as gas will expand to fill all the space available, so troubles of any size will occupy the whole of our being. If you let a little gas out of your stove's burner, you will soon be able to smell it all over the room. Let a little problem into your mind, and soon you will not be thinking of anything else.

Our own experience verifies this. One day we are irritated by a "snippy" clerk, and that is all we can think about. All the way home we go over the remarks made, think of what we should have said, consider calling the manager and getting her fired. We are completely absorbed by this petty irritation. The next day we are called by the school nurse, our child is ill. All the way to school we think of all the diseases it might be, where to find the doctor, whether to go to the emergency room. Our whole mind is wrapped up in this important problem. Whether troubles are little or large, like gas, they fill the rooms of our lives.

The small problems are usually overcome when they are pushed out of the way by larger ones, either our own or others. I have heard people in hospital beds say they did not know when they were well off. I have also had the experience of coming into the hospital, absorbed in some petty personal problem, and finding in the patients' much larger pain that I have forgotten my own.

But there ought to be a better way. Perhaps Dr. Frankl's analogy can help us. If trouble, like a gas, spreads out to fill the whole space available to it, then perhaps the answer is just to give our troubles no more space than they really need. How long should one really be bothered by a snippy clerk? How important is it, truly, that we missed the bus? And why should we let our whole soul be disturbed by trouble which ought to be put in a box the right size?

Your troubles will expand like gas to fill all the room available. Just do not give them any more room than they need.

Suppose you could swap your troubles

Another way of getting perspective on our troubles is to compare them to the next fellow's.

We can all profit by an old story. It seems that God grew tired of listening to man's wails of woe. Each human being was crying to the Lord that he was the most miserable of men, that his misfortunes were far greater than those of others, that he was carrying more than his share of life's troubles. So God said, "All of you come out to the public square, and bring your troubles in a sack with you, and there hang them all out on clotheslines where all can be seen. Then I am going to let you exchange troubles. If you like someone else's problems better, I'll let you have them; you can take them home in place of your own."

And so it was that the next day the people brought their troubles to the public square and hung them out on lines. When the Lord gave a signal to exchange troubles, every man ran quickly to his own, stuffed them back into his sack, and went home satisfied.

Surely we all have troubles, big ones, but they are no worse than the next man's.

I recall seeing some men with big problems. They were part of Horace Heidt's orchestra. One of them was a blind xylophonist who played an immensely complicated number almost without an error, even though he had to be led to and from his musical instrument. The other performer was a tap dancer who had lost a leg on Okinawa, and yet was able to give us a tap dance of unusual skill and perfect timing, and I still do not know which leg was artificial.

As I watched these two men, I am honest enough to say that I cried. There were salty tears in my eyes, and a lump in my throat. To think of the glory of the human spirit which could so triumph over handicaps. What sort of strength, what sort of grit and determination they must have had to go through the weeks and months of literally grueling practice? Can you imagine playing a xylophone with its two banks of keys without the gift of sight? Can you imagine the frustration of making one mistake after another in practice and literally perspiring over every note, if you could neither see the music nor the instrument? Or can you imagine controlling an artificial limb sufficiently to go through the intricate routine of tap dancing? How many times he must have fallen. How many times he must have faltered. How many times he must have cursed the day he was wounded. And yet, these two men, ordinary men like you and me, triumphed in the battle of life and succeeded in mastering their inadequacies, in training their afflicted bodies to perform skillfully arts which even a whole body finds difficult.

And I thought to myself that day, and I have thought many times since, what if we whose bodies are whole and healthy, what if we whose eyes are strong and clear, would put even one tenth as much effort as they did into mastering the arts of life, what great characters we could develop.

Surely to control a bad temper should be no more difficult than to control an artificial leg. Surely to see good in every person we meet should not be more difficult than to play a xylophone with unseeing eyes.

And yet, how we coddle ourselves, and excuse ourselves, and find a hundred reasons why we are as we are. The fact is we are simply lazy. We don't want to work at the development of character. We do not want to discipline our natures. We do not want to learn how to get along with people, how to be kind, considerate, helpful, or noble. We baby ourselves, and spoil ourselves, and lose so much of life's value just because we are unwilling to submit to the rigid self-discipline which alone can produce a life worth living.

And either we ought to admit it, or else we ought to do something about it. Either we ought to say frankly to ourselves, "I could quit being so ugly to my employees, but I do not want to," or else to set about improving our relationships with them. Either we ought to say honestly, "I could give my children more understanding and more patient love, but I do not want to," or else begin training ourselves to give that understanding and love.

Because (I say it again) if these men, handicapped as they are, could develop the skills and the aptitudes which they demonstrated on Horace Heidt's program, then there are no limits to the human spirit and no real obstacles to human achievement. We can become what we want to become. We can realize our highest dreams of ourselves.

The hardest of all tasks

I do sometimes think, however, that big problems may be easier to handle than small ones. A Bible verse from Isaiah would seem to indicate this.

"They who wait for the Lord shall mount up with wings like eagles;
they shall run and not be weary;
they shall walk and not faint."

At first glance, I once read, these phrases seem to be in reverse order. In normal speech, we go from the lesser to the greater, and therefore it would be better form to say, "They shall walk and not be faint, run without wearying, yea, mount on eagle's wings."

But Isaiah had something else in mind than speed. He was thinking of difficulty. The hardest task in all of life is to walk and not be faint. In life's crises when we must fly, in life's challenging hours when we must run, we rise to the occasion, we find the strength; but plodding day after weary day is the hard thing.

I heard a wife complaining of her husband. He neglected her and their children shamefully. "And yet," she went on to say, "when any of us is sick, he is the most wonderful husband and father anyone could want." He could run; he could not walk.

Parents understand this. When a baby cries in pain, we find the strength to carry it for hour after hour. Let a child need medical care, and we will give up sleep, mortgage the house, do anything to heal. But oh, that daily round of sterilizing bottles and washing diapers—that's what gets us down.

Ministers have the same problem. It's a wonderful thing to stand up and preach. It's a great experience to go to the hospital in the dead of night and give a spiritual transfusion to some sick soul. But the daily labor, the writing of a bulletin, conferences on the color of the pulpit cloth, smoothing over a quarrel between committee members—this is when the soul grows faint.

What Isaiah was trying to say, therefore, was this: They who wait for the Lord, they who have a deep faith, will receive from God not only the power to mount up on eagles' wings, not only the strength to meet life's critical demands, but the power to walk without faintness, to have zest and purpose in the dull tasks of daily life.

What holds the kite up?

The responsibilities for the daily task are not all liability. While flying a kite, I once asked my father, "Dad, what holds the kite up?"

"The string," he replied.

"No, Dad, the string holds it down, not up."

"If you think so, let go of the string," he said, "and see what happens."

I let go and the kite began to fall!

It seems odd that the very thing which seems to keep the kite down is actually what keeps it up. And this is true not only of kites but of life. Those strings that are tied to us, those rules and regulations that seem to us to hold us down, are actually holding us up!

When we were youngsters, we used to fret about all the things that hampered us, the parents and teachers who were constantly saying no. But then vacation would come when we were no longer tied down but free as air, and after a few weeks, we used to wonder what to do and how to spend our time.

Most of us have seen this demonstrated in the life of some carefree, footloose, irresponsible youth who never hangs up his clothes, never has a dollar left in his pocket, but is blown one way and then another by the winds of life. Then he marries and has a baby, and suddenly tied down, he becomes an upright, responsible and considerate husband, father, citizen. All he needed was some cord to hold him up.

And certainly in the realm of the spirit, in the field of faith, this same truth holds with even greater force. The word "religion" is said to come from a Latin root meaning "to hold back" or "tie back." And this is what religion does. It provides the string to the soaring kite of our spirit; it keeps us from falling. It binds us to great values; it attaches us to great causes; it helps us fly high in the air of God's truth and lifts us until our heads touch the stars and our lives take on the beauty and the glory of men and women who are bound closely to God.

Take your licking

Living with our problems also involves facing our responsibilities.

Former President Harry S. Truman used to have a little placard on his desk, I am told, that reads: THE BUCK STOPS HERE. What a wonderful way it was to indicate where the final authority rested.

It would seem to me that each of us needs this motto for that inner desk where we keep our moral accounts, for we do tend to pass the buck of moral responsibility to others. We need to realize that *the buck stops here* in each of our souls.

It is amazing how often people try to escape responsibility for their actions. Children's excuses are always so transparent, but with just a little insight, we can see our own.

A child says, "He started it." A businessman says, "My competitor was doing it. It was either follow suit or go out of business."

A child says, "The teacher is a creep." The college student says, "The instructor didn't make it relevant."

A child says, "Why did you let me?" A grownup says, "My parents spoiled me."

We do pass the buck for our delinquencies to our parents, our teachers, our neighbors. Always *they* failed, *they* stumbled, *they* did wrong.

Freud's original theory gave mankind a whole new set of excuses. Freud viewed the human personality as somewhat mechanical—this cause produced that effect. He once suggested that if you deprived a group of men of their freedom, of food, and the like for a certain length of time, you could reduce all of them to the same primitive level. But in Korea we discovered that under the very same conditions, different prisoners reacted in different ways. Some became subhuman and some became heroes. Some lost all pride, some walked in dignity. Each man, facing life and its problems, must choose; and no one else chooses for him. He can follow the crowd, or he can go it alone. He can give in to his appetites or say no to them. No theory can rob man of his moral freedom.

The buck stops here.

And because it does, we would do well to accept the consequences of our mistakes. One good rule would be to "take your licking before you get in too deep." I do not know where

I first heard or read that sentence, but it is a wise one. "Take your licking before you get in too deep."

The ideal time to apply these words would be when a child has done something and is asked who did it. Many children will deny everything, and then reinforce the denial by telling a whole series of lies until they are enmeshed in their own trap, and are punished doubly both for doing wrong and for lying. Can't you hear a father in that situation saying to his son, "Take your licking before you get in too deep."

But this is not the only situation in which these words apply. Too many of us do not know when to stop.

A man sits down at a poker table and begins to lose. Soon he is betting larger sums to win back his losses, and before the evening is over, he has lost more heavily than he can afford. He should have taken his licking before he got in too deep.

A man borrows a little money from the cash register to cover a hospital bill for a sick wife; then he falsifies the figures to cover the theft, steals a little more to invest in the stock market so that with the profits he can replace his first theft, and the market goes down. He should have taken his licking before he got in too deep.

Sometimes a couple find their marriage cracking up, and they decide in desperation that maybe having a child will bring them back together. So they gamble their marriage on a baby, and they lose—but the baby pays the debt. Now I would not advise any couple to secure a divorce, but if their marriage is crumbling, then better a divorce than a baby to be raised in a broken home. If you have to take a licking, take it before you get others in too deep.

Men walk the streets with bad colds. Suggest to them that they go to bed for a day or two, and they will scoff at you—nothing to it, just a sniffle—and then they are under oxygen with pneumonia. They would not take their licking, and they got in too deep.

Do we not find an instance in the Bible? Pharaoh could not

stop—for five plagues in a row he hardened his heart, and then for five more plagues God hardened it for him, and so, instead of one licking, he took ten bad strokes ending with the death of his very own son.

There is a profound moral truth in this matter. It has to do with the whole development of character. The man who refuses to take his licking, who will not admit his weakness, his failure, his wrongdoing or his foolishness, is like a person who struggles in quicksand; the more he thrashes about, the more quickly he is swallowed up. But let him realize that he is caught, and throw himself upon the mercy of the court, as it were, before he gets in too deep, before he reaches the point of no return, and he may be saved, his wrong may be expiated, his mistake may be corrected, and his feet put back upon the paths of useful and happy living.

One way to get out of trouble is to call for help. But it has been my observation that many people call on their ministers for help too late.

Much of the time we ministers are the "last ditch" effort of people in trouble. I recall a book title which implied the same thing; it was called *Why Not Try God?* And that is the way it frequently is. People in trouble, people with worries and anxieties and problems will talk to their parents, to their in-laws, to cousins, uncles, aunts, and to perfect strangers, and brood over their cares by day and by night, and then when things have gone so far that it is almost impossible to unravel the knot or get things back to normal, in they come hoping perhaps the minister has a magic word that will make it all go away.

This is most frequently the case with a couple who are quarreling. They fight, argue, separate and make up, and separate again; they talk to their friends, and the friends talk to them and try to bring them together again, and finally, when they feel that they just cannot take it any more, that the whole game is up, they seek their lawyer to begin divorce proceedings, and he, most of the time, will say, "Now, before you start getting a divorce, why don't you talk to your minister?" And then they come, and at that last ditch seek out their religious leader for help.

Most of the time, unfortunately, it is too late. A bad marital relationship is something like a cancer—catch it early, diagnose and treat it, and you are likely to live a long, healthy life. Catch it too late, and all you can do is ease the suffering. So with breaking homes. Sometimes the first rift is a simple little misunderstanding, a failure in communication, an inability to talk something over, or perhaps it grew out of an in-law problem, or a question of ruffled feelings that never got unruffled. This happens in all marriages, and most of us find a way to patch up the rift, make up the quarrel, and go on to greater understanding. But if a couple do not manage to work out this first serious difference, then it becomes a sort of running sore or cancerous growth, which can ultimately eat away their happiness and destroy their marriage. It is when they do not manage to solve their *first* serious difference that they need to go to their minister or some other counsellor who can advise them.

What they usually discover, if they take the trouble, is that their quarrel is rather standard, that they need to make certain changes in attitude, or behavior, and can easily do so.

The same thing is true in many of life's other problems. Parents watch some ugly habit or trait grow in a child. They try this and that, they talk about it and worry about it, and hope that it will go away. Perhaps it does seem to yield to treatment for a while, but so often they wait too long, and then have a full-grown juvenile delinquent on their hands.

So a child, growing up, will see his relationship to his parents begin to get complicated, and he does not know how to cut the apron strings. To please mama and not worry papa, he undertakes certain ways of life, or gives up certain choices he might have had, and suddenly finds that he is deep in emotional trouble when it's almost too late.

Above all, our help in carrying our responsibilities and facing our problems can come from God. It was to Him that Moses turned and cried, "Why have you laid the burden of this people upon me? Did I conceive them? Did I bring them forth? I am not able to carry them alone."

The authentic voice of the human heart is here heard. Who has not felt it, or seen it? Sometimes you can sense it in the face of the President of the United States—too much responsibility, too much criticism, too many crises—"I cannot carry this people by myself."

Sometimes you see it in the face of a doctor late at night, after a day when so many have depended upon him, pushed him and pulled him to heal their aches and soothe their hearts.

You may recall it in your own life. What wife and mother has not, after a winter of constant illness, when it has rained every washday, and a grumpy husband wants to know when supper is ready—what wife has not suddenly cried, "I cannot carry this burden alone."

But somehow Moses found the strength to carry on. "Is God's arm too short?" he heard Him say. Renewed in faith, he recovered his patience, his courage, his hope.

And so with us. How many people have told me what a wonderful thing it is to walk into that oasis of peace in God's house at the end of the week, take the great burden of troubles off one's shoulders, and "complain" a little to God, and then, in His presence find that while the troubles are no lighter, the shoulders are stronger.

Like Moses, who in bitterness cried out, "I cannot carry this people alone," and then found that he did not have to, so we, with the same cry, find the same answer.

We learn from hardship

Life's problems add to life's liveliness. Arnold Toynbee, the great historian, wrote in the *Woman's Home Companion* of August, 1949, a story about fishermen on the east coast of

England. Their problem was to keep the herring they caught
alive until they were able to get them to market. It seemed
that dead herring soon turned flabby and tasteless, and so
fishermen began to build salt water tanks in their fishing
boats, and would dump the herring they caught out of the
nets into those tanks so as to keep them alive until they
could bring them to port. But the herring soon realized that
they were prisoners in the small tank; there was no place to
go, and so they turned very listless and sluggish.

One fishing boat captain discovered a trick by which to
keep his catch not merely alive but lively and interested in
life, so that they were in excellent condition for the market.
He told his secret to a friend of Mr. Toynbee's one day. "It
is really very simple," he said. "I put a catfish in my tank,
and that catfish can be trusted to keep the herring lively.
To be sure, he will eat one or two of them on the way to
port, but that is the catfish's wages. And he is worth his
keep, because those herring do come in fresh, and the price
they fetch on the market pays for the catfish's toll more than
fifty times over."

The moral is obvious. We develop strong teeth, not by eating pablum, but by chewing on tough crusts. We develop
strong minds, not by idling and day dreaming, but by tackling work that takes hard mental labor. We develop strong
characters, not in the days when the going is easy, but
when temptation and trouble makes the going rough.

Some of the most beautiful flowering plants come from
hothouses. But transplant them out in the yard, expose them
to the weather, and they often die on the stalk. They've had it
too easy. Controlled temperature, rich plant food. They can't
"take it."

You have met hothouse personalities who were lovely and
charming in life's gay and happy hours, but who went to
pieces in the face of some of life's greater problems.

Children who have had everything they want, who have
never had to go without or do without, so often turn into

flabby grownups. Youngsters with good brains have some-times let theirs minds go to seed because they never had to study.

Of course, deliberately to let loose the catfish of life in order to train our children, or educate ourselves, would be cruel. But, on the other hand, we ought to recognize that illness and hard luck, bad times and tragedy, are not all loss. I have seen young people, who could best be called scatter-brained, suddenly grow up when family needs required their maturing.

I saw this happen frequently with soldiers I had known as civilians. We hear so much about service-connected disabili-ties; I wonder that no one has ever given much thought to service-connected *abilities*.

Most of the men with whom I served as chaplain overseas will tell you that while they would not want to go through it again, they would not have missed it for a million! And why? Because their years in uniform added to their abilities. They learned many a truth about life, added many a capacity to their character.

They learned to face fear. Once a man has looked death in the eye through days and nights of danger, he knows that never again will he be afraid. He may be frightened, but he will not fear. He has met the test of courage. I have seen frightened boys turn into men of true valor. This is a service-connected ability.

There are others. Once a man has lived together with a company of soldiers, he will never again judge men by ex-ternals. Everywhere else in life, men are judged by appear-ances, by the kind of clothes they wear to work, by their neighborhood, their school tie, the size of their bank account, their house of worship, their mother's maiden name. But in the Army, a man is just a man; he is judged by his own ability, personality, character. And he learns to judge others by the same standard. He is not fooled by appearances, nor cowed by authority. He sees men for what they truly are. This, too, is a service-connected ability.

The catfish keeps the herring lively. Our hardships can do the same for us.

We might sum it all up in one phrase. *We cannot determine the fall of the cards, but we can determine how to play the hand.* Anyone who has played cards (even Old Maid) will understand what this means. When the deck is shuffled and the cards are dealt, the hand a person gets, whether good or bad, is beyond his control. And yet, how many different ways we can play the hand we get. Some of us grumble, slap each card angrily on the table, even throw in our hands and stamp away. Others crow with each card won, curse every loss. But the good cardplayer is the one who takes the cards as they come, plays them quietly and carefully, and wins or loses without an outcry.

So it is in life. We cannot determine the fall of the cards. We do not know what the future holds for us, whether health or illness, prosperity or poverty, family unity or sorrow. The cards have all been shuffled and all we can do is wait till they are dealt and pick up our hand. But we can determine how we play our hands. If illness comes, we can grumble and whine or face it with radiant mental health. If riches come, we can gloat or we can share; if poverty, we can complain or we can endure. If grief comes, we can take it as a personal insult from God or with deep faith in His providence. These choices are ours.

Our prayer will naturally be for a hand full of "good cards," but it should include also a heart full of strength and character. Because whether our life will be a happy one will depend not on the hand we hold, but on the way we play our cards.

10

Living with Suffering and Grief

"How can you say God loves us," asked my cynical friend, "when you see pain and poverty, sickness and suffering, defeat and death?"

Does the fact that we suffer mean that God really does not care? I do not think so. He is our Father, and He wants us to learn to walk uprightly. Human parents can understand this. When a baby takes its first step we crow with delight. This is part of its growth. Yet, in learning to walk, babies fall down. Nature usually cushions that fall, but sometimes babies topple sidewise, perhaps hit their head on some sharp corner, and are hurt. Could a baby, hurt in this fashion, accuse his parents of not loving him? And what shall we parents do? Carry a child all his life that he may never fall and be hurt?

Parents put a baby in a playpen with another, tell him and show him about co-operation and sharing and love, but sometimes a little hand snatches something the other baby wants, or a little fist reaches out and a cry of pain goes up. Does this prove that parents do not love their children? We human parents love our children very much, but we know that they have to learn to live with people, and sometimes they can get hurt.

The fact that sometimes we suffer does not mean that God does not care. He has given us a moral sense and freedom to walk uprightly, and this means we can hurt ourselves and hurt each other. But when we do, God is concerned and He is still there. He heals the sick and comforts the mourner.

Who of us has not known this? All of us have had the experience of looking out of eyes blinded with grief into a darkness blacker than midnight, and then suddenly in the far distance, seeing the glimmer of His light. God does care.

Actually, the Twenty-third Psalm says this. It does not claim that life is all green pastures, all quiet waters. There will be shadows, evil, and death, but we shall not fear, for He is with us. We may not know why the world is so constructed that babies, learning to walk, sometimes fall, and men, learning to walk uprightly, will also sometimes fall, but this we know: God loves us, and helps us to pick ourselves up again and walk on with Him.

There is more that we need to learn. Life's clouds and shadows may be very unpleasant, yet even they can have a value if we see them in the right perspective.

On one summer's vacation, I had the chance to watch the sun set every night for a month. And I discovered something I had never realized before. The sun setting by itself is not particularly beautiful. Not at all. It is only beautiful if there are clouds. When the sun is all alone in the sky, then the light of day fades as when they dim the lights in a theater, calmly and quietly, but not beautifully. But if there are any clouds at all, any place in the sky, to the west or east or north or south, then the sunset becomes a thing of beauty. The light flames orange in the west, in the east there are pink and vivid white, in the south the clouds are the color of gold, and to the north are violet shadows. It is clouds that make a sunset lovely.

It is clouds that make life's sky beautiful, too. Our human happiness is given color and joy by clouds of pain, of trouble, of sorrow.

Hasn't this been your experience? Look back through your life and recall the clouds that made the sunlight more beautiful. It may have been illness. We take our health so for granted. It takes an ache and a pain to remind us of the blessings of health. A man once told me that the best thing that ever happened to him was his heart attack. "I wasn't living before," he said. "Life was just a routine. I had my nose to the grindstone and just never looked up. But now I'm living. Every morning is a new and fresh day. Every sight of my children and grandchildren is a precious moment. I see beauty where I never saw it before." Here is a life made beautiful by a cloud.

It may have been in time of accident, sorrow, tragedy that you suddenly discovered the kindness of human hearts and the meaning of friendship. People whose homes have burned can tell you what real neighborliness means, and how the flood of fellow feeling warmed their hearts. When tragedy strikes, friends you haven't seen for years come to give their hand in sympathy. Let two automobiles collide, and perfect strangers will endanger their lives to rescue you, go out of their way to help you, shine like sunlight on the clouds of your trouble.

No one wants cloudy days. No one seeks trouble or sorrow. But when they come, they bring beauty with them.

Tears are the price of love

Grief is the kind of trouble that seems hardest to bear.

A gullible friend of mine once sent off a dime and a self-addressed envelope for a *sure-fire* prescription for avoiding falling hair! The reply came on a prescription blank, "To avoid falling hair, step nimbly aside."

Would you like to have a prescription for avoiding grief? Here it is: "Just avoid love."

In time of sorrow, people ask the age-old question, "Why do we suffer so? Why should we have to grieve? Why does God do this to us?"

There is no answer concerning those who have gone except the answer of faith: God knows what He is about; even if we cannot understand His actions, they are part of His plan.

But there is an answer to those who remain behind and mourn. Tears are the price of love. If you would not weep, do not love. Avoid all human ties. Give up your parents, do not marry, have no children, seek no friends. Seal off your heart from all companionship, all concern, all affection. Then it won't hurt when they fall sick or die. You just won't care, and tears need never furrow your cheek.

But if you would have love in your life, then know for sure that you or they will mourn and grieve. As our synagogue prayer book puts it, "Tears are the tribute of tender yearning for those who have passed away but cannot be forgotten."

Tears are the price of love. And after all, it is worth it, is it not?

When a life that is full of years and rich in character comes to its end, men ought not to mourn. At least, this is what one Talmudic rabbi suggested, and he developed a parable to prove his point.

When a ship is launched, it is a joyful occasion. Flags fly and bands play when a boat slides down the ways into the sea. But as much joy as there is at its launching (and remember, this rabbi wrote in the days of small sailing vessels), how much more there is when a ship comes safely home, for it means that the storms have been weathered and all the lurking dangers of the sea successfully surmounted! Yes, there is joy at a launching and joy at homecoming.

So, too, with a human life. We launch it happily; our hearts swell with pride as a new baby sets sail on the seas of life. And how dangerous those seas! How many storms, how many shoals, how many perils! How wonderful if the ship of life can weather all the storms and finally, laden with treasure, sail into God's haven. We should not mourn, said the rabbi of olden days.

Of course, we cannot help grieving. It is painful to give up our loved ones, no matter how long they have lived. But the parable of the boat should help us rise above our grief and, beyond our tears, feel solemn joy at the successful completion of life's voyage.

Not long ago, I laid to rest a lovely woman whose life had been most happy and most useful. She was loved by her children; she was adored by her grandchildren. One of the hardest problems for the family was to break the news of her death to the tiny grandchildren who had been closest to her in life, to tell them of the passing of the grandmother whom they called "momma." But their fears were groundless. The tiny granddaughter did not go into any paroxysm of grief. On the contrary, with the profound wisdom of childhood, she listened gravely, she thought a moment, and then she said, "That's all right. Don't you worry. We've got pictures of momma."

How could it be put more clearly? How better could anyone be comforted, or comfort another? Death is not the end of our love; we have pictures.

I know this from my own life. Sometimes, looking through a family album, I come suddenly upon pictures of my own grandmothers (may their memory be for blessing). And when I look at those faded snapshots, the floodgates of memory open. I can recall the wonderful noodle soup that delighted a child's heart; I can remember the open prayer book and the lips moving in silent devotion; I can remember the long drives with them on a summer evening; and so much more. They are still alive for me; I have pictures.

Of course, the real pictures are not in the album. They are in the heart. The photographs simply stimulate the moving pictures of memory. It is what they were, not how they looked, that stays with us. We have pictures not just of their faces, but of their character, their sweetness, their love.

The death of a child

Of all life's tragedies, the most pitiful is the death of a child. We know that in the order of nature we will one day stand at our parents' graveside, but to lose a child brings anguish beyond words.

The Talmud tells a story of how a brave wife helped her husband face their children's death. Meir and Beruriah had twin sons whom they loved with all their hearts. One summer day, they both were taken ill and within the hour had died. When Meir came home in the evening, his first question was of his sons. "Why haven't they run to meet me as they usually do?"

"They are upstairs," said Beruriah, "but before you go up, I need your advice. Years ago, a man came and left some jewels with me for safekeeping. They were beautiful gems and I have grown to love them very much. Today, without any advance notice, the man returned and demanded his jewels. Must I give them up?"

"Of course you must," said Meir. Without another word, his wife led him to the room where the boys lay dead. "My jewels, my jewels," cried Meir, "the Lord has given, the Lord has taken."

Through the years this story has brought comfort to many a heart. We do not know why God calls some early and others late. We only know that our lives are in His hand, our loved ones a loan from Him. And when He takes them away, we can only echo what Meir and Beruriah said. We can only thank Him for the few precious years of love and laughter whose memory will warm our hearts forever.

Another brave woman who can help others who have lost a child is Helen Chappel White. Although I read it years ago, I have never forgotten her book, *With Wings as Eagles*. She had lost her son in war and after months of bitter mourning, finally made her peace with death. I do not think that any book I have read (except the Bible) could better help those whose grief seems unbearable.

The nub of it is contained in this paragraph: "Eventually I saw, almost with horror, that this 'loyalty' of mine had led me to a final treachery; the hurt of having lost him had at last outweighed the joy of having had him, and the sadness of his death had dimmed for me the happiness of his life."

In seeking to comfort people in sorrow, which is one of every minister's major tasks, I have recalled these words frequently, especially with those whose grief is caused by untimely death. Most of us are capable of accepting the death of the aged; their time has come, and we know that soon or late we must lose them. But when the young die, when a wife must bury her husband, or parents their children, then Mrs. White's words help me comfort the bereaved.

Frequently people will nurse their sorrow, moisten the funeral flowers with their tears to keep them alive, seek to demonstrate and to prove their love by their sorrow.

It is for this reason that, in due season, people should be led from speaking of their sorrow to recalling their joys. Ask to see a family album and pictures of happy occasions. Talk of days of courtship when a mate is lost, or baby days when a child has gone, because these are what can give grief its outlet and help the "joy of having had him overcome the grief of having lost him."

Grief is a natural thing, and woe to those who lock it up within themselves and refuse to let themselves go. But to grow out of grief is a necessary thing, and it can best be done by replacing the memories of the days of pain with the memories of the days of joy. It is this that is implied in the phrase: "May the memories of our loved ones be for blessing." They can, if we let them.

The sum of it is this: there is no life without its tears, but if there were, it would be missing a lot of its laughter, too. Because shadows bring out light.

One evening, on vacation in the hill country, I sat looking out at the quiet evening when suddenly, as though the hand of some great painter had splashed color on a canvas, some hills seemed to "leap out" from the distant landscape. I had not seen them before. They had been there, but they had been like the background of wallpaper, a monotone of color.

But when the long slanting rays of the evening sun began to highlight the hill tops and purple the valleys, the beauty appeared. And then it was that I understood fully what I once heard a photographer say: "Don't take pictures at mid-day —the sunlight washes out the shadows. It takes shadows to make beauty."

In life, too, happiness is highlighted by the shadows of pain and sorrow. Real happiness, that is. When we are overwhelmed with grief and trouble, we think we would settle for a world without laughter if only we could also have it without tears. In the long perspective of maturity, however, we come more and more to recognize that there is no beauty without shadows and no happiness without sorrow, and we accept the joys gladly even when we know they have a price.

Families who face grief are brought more closely together. A couple who have had to economize in the early years of marriage enjoy the better days that follow. A person who has known a disappointment is all the more joyous for an achievement.

I feel sure that no one will take this so seriously as to go out looking for troubles so as to increase pleasure. This would be like hitting yourself on the head with a hammer because it feels so good when you quit. But it can give a perspective in which, when pain comes, we accept it without resentment and bitterness. For in the long run, life's tragedies highlight life's victory; life's shadows give it its beauty.

III

Living with Your Family

1

The Key to True Happiness

The family is the key to personal growth and happiness. The human baby must have the love and the care of his parents (or their substitutes) to grow physically, to mature psychologically, and to develop spiritually. Without that love and without that care, it has been proved in study after study, he is less resistant to disease, less secure in mental health, less mature in moral responsibilities. The psychiatrists' couches are littered with the debris of broken families. Without a happy home, all the other joys of life are empty.

The family is also the foundation of human society. The love and mutual obligations which bind husband to wife, parents to children, and generation to generation are the stones upon which all else is built. No one has ever found a substitute for the family. When the family decays, therefore, nations decay; when family life declines, nations decline; when the family goes, civilization goes. This is re-emphasized by one of the blessings at a Jewish wedding, "May Jerusalem rejoice in the happiness of her sons and daughters." A city's joy and strength are built on the joy and strength of its family life. The broken home leads to the broken nation.

From this point of view, America is in a bad way. There were 400,000 divorces in the United States in 1961 (which is proportionately three to four times as many as in almost any European nation). There are at this moment more than fifteen million American men and women who have been divorced. There are more than four million children under eighteen years of age who are children of broken homes. And sociologists predict that, if the past is any indication of the future, of all the marriages contracted this year, one out of four will end in the divorce court.

Therefore, for our own sakes and for the sake of our children, and for the sake of our country and our world, we need to learn to live with our families.

As a rabbi, I feel that perhaps I have a special contribution to make to this subject. The Jewish family has been widely praised as an example of family life at its best. Judges, social workers, psychologists, have repeatedly referred to the close-knit quality of the Jewish family, the tenderness of man and wife, the co-operative affection of brothers and sisters, the low delinquency rate of its youngsters, the warm care of aged parents. Mark Twain, in an unusually serious vein, wrote: "The Jewish home is a home in the truest sense. The family is knitted together by the strongest affections; its members show each other every due respect."

And when we examine that Jewish home, and the principles upon which it is built, and then turn to the conclusions of modern social scientists, we find a remarkable similarity.

Four marriage principles of Judaism

Scholars of the past have summarized the principles of Judaism as they apply to home life in four terms. The Jewish home is marked by purity in the relationship of man and wife, by loving responsibility for the welfare and education of the children, by affectionate respect for the dignity and security of parents, and by a loyalty to the *family as a whole*.

Let me amplify on these values.

Family purity was based on a deep respect for the physical relationship between man and woman, a relationship that was to be treated neither with vulgarity nor prudery. It was built on monogamy. Although the Bible recognized polygamy, the Talmud, which also permitted it, records not a single sage as having more than one wife, and one of them remarked that "if God had intended Adam to have many wives, he would have taken many ribs." And above all, the Jewish family was based on a single standard, chastity before marriage and absolute fidelity after it for both men and women.

The responsibility of parents for the welfare and education of their children was spelled out in every detail. The physical, social, educational, and religious needs of youngsters could not be referred to others. A child's grades in school, his moral behavior, his diet were watched like a hawk. Many a Jewish child has said of his mother, "She breathed for me."

The honoring of parents was equally important. To respect the wishes of parents, to preserve their dignity in old age, to care for them in helplessness was the response of children to the love of parents.

And the concept of family loyalty wove together all of these privileges and responsibilities into one emotional fabric called in Hebrew, *Sholom Bais*. The translation, "the peace of the home," cannot quite describe the combination of independence and interdependence in which each individual was encouraged to grow to his highest, and at the same time expected to reflect honor upon and to share his good fortune with the family as a whole.

And these four characteristics of Jewish home life were strengthened by the home-centered character of much of Jewish religious practice. The communal faith of the synagogue was important, but it was supplemented by the sanctuary of the home. The table worship each Friday evening, the special foods on each festival and holy day, and above all, the Passover Seder which was an occasion of family reunion from far and near, reinforced the purity, the affection, and the mutual love that gave the Jewish home its strength.

If you turn now to books written by contemporary sociologists and psychologists on the family and study those chapters that attempt to describe a good family, a healthy family, or an ideal family, you will find certain ideas repeated in every book. They include mutual affection, agreement on values, agreement on child-rearing, emotional interdependence, and family celebrations and ceremonies. What are these values but precisely those which the Jewish family has evolved through the ages as its patterns of a secure and stable family life?

It is where these two strands meet, tradition and research, Judaism and sociology, that we begin to seek lessons for living with our family.

2

Romance Isn't Enough

The first great weakness in the contemporary family is in our attitude toward romance and courtship.

The patterns of modern courtship are rather new. Young people may be surprised to know, but it's not so many generations ago that the idea of asking a girl for a date, of going out without a chaperone, of being allowed to "choose" a wife, was fairly unusual. Courtship might have begun with seeing someone who appealed to you. Then you'd go home and say to your father, "Please talk to her father." Often parents alone would meet at a social affair or at the market and there they would "arrange" a marriage. Or a matchmaker, a man skilled in recognizing the similarities in family backgrounds, age, and temperament, would match couples. You might meet for the first time at the engagement party, "Here's your future wife." You met again a year later at the wedding. Our young people hold up their hands in dismay. "How could this ever have been? How could they possibly marry somebody they didn't know, someone they hadn't dated, hadn't gone steady with, 'pinned,' 'dropped,' and finally ringed?" But they did it. And it worked pretty well. The Jewish family, so full of love and warmth and charm, was often built by couples who never courted.

Modern courtship grows out of medieval romantic chivalry when knighthood was in flower and when men would sigh gusty sighs over their beloved and carry handkerchiefs to battle with them (very frequently some other man's wife's handkerchief). But romantic love had very little to do with social obligations, very little to do with comradeship, with friendship. It was a game and this mating game of knights and their ladies has somehow given us the pattern of modern courtship and romantic love.

Now I do not object to romantic love, but to assume that it is the all of love is a dangerous half-truth, and like most half-truths ends up in becoming completely false.

In my counseling I hear romantic love used as the excuse for every foolishness, and the solution to every problem.

A young couple in romantic love will step across the boundaries of proper behavior. Troubles follow and I ask, "How did you get into this situation?" "We loved each other" comes the answer, "and when people love each other, how can this be wrong?" *But it is wrong, and no amount of love will make it right!*

A young couple, romantically in love, sit down with me to discuss their marriage. It is apparent from the very beginning that there are tremendous obstacles to their successful marriage, differences in education or background, or religion, differences about *which they are already quarreling*, but they will say with bland assurance, "We believe that if two people love each other enough, they can solve any problem."

It is not so. Problems cannot be solved by love alone. It takes so much more, some intelligence, some unselfishness, some self-control. And too often instead of love solving the problems, the problems dissolve the love. In many breaking marriages, the things that are wrong have been wrong since the day they met each other, and they have known it all along. But they believed, because society told them so, that if you just love each other enough, you can solve all problems. Love may be a wonderful climate for problem-solving, but problems are not solved by love alone.

There's still another effect of this half-truth. If a couple marry each other with this burning sensation in the heart, this wild romantic love, and if then the romantic love fades, there seems really to be no point in the marriage; it becomes almost "immoral" to be married to someone you don't love in romantic fashion. And suppose you "fall" for someone else? When the honeymoon's over, and life becomes a little humdrum, and the hero unbuttons his collar and the heroine puts on curl papers, romantic love flies out the window, so to speak, and the marriage comes to an end.

And what is perhaps worst of all, it seems to me, is the fact that this concept of romantic love emphasizes everything that's shallow and everything that's superficial in what really makes a marriage go. It has to do with physical appeal, with glamour and with beauty, and these things fade. I know that youngsters look at their parents, balding and sagging, and wonder how they could love each other, because love is supposed to be romantic and glamorous and beautiful.

It takes more than a union of bodies

What we've done is emphasize the art of love-making instead of the art of homemaking. We put physical relationships first in a marriage; we put them first in getting married and we put them first in getting divorced. But marriage is not just mating, it's much more. And marriage is not just a union of bodies, it's a union of hearts and souls and of minds. Without this higher union, there is no true love; there is only romancing.

In seeking to communicate such a philosophy, a parable from the Hebrew is of high value. The words for man and woman in the Hebrew language, *Eysh* and *Eshah,* have some letters in common and some which are not shared. *E* and *sh* are found in both, *y* and *ah* are in only one of the two. Now it so happens that *Esh* means fire, and that *Yah* means God. The meaning of this Hebrew footnote is quite plain. Unless a man and a woman, attracted to each other by the fires of passion, add God to their relationship, their love will go up in smoke.

That a couple feel attracted to each other is vital to their marriage. Without it, there can be little affection or love. But they must also both be attracted to mutual values, to divine truth as well. A marriage, a good marriage, is built on a sharing of dreams, and of goals. When a couple have deep differences about the purpose of life and its destiny, about God and about man's duties to God, then the flames of passion will flicker and die.

And the important thing about this kind of love is that it doesn't have to begin with great romance. There's a lovely story in the Bible that all of you recall, the story of Isaac and Rebecca. Isaac didn't call up Rebecca in Aramea and ask for a date. Eleazar was sent by Abraham: "Find a good wife for my son—somebody of my people, somebody who shares our values." And when Eleazar went, he didn't have a beauty contest to find out the loveliest, he had a camel-watering contest. He chose the finest, the gentlest, the most generous, and he brought her back. And the story ends in the most beautiful fashion: "And Isaac took Rebecca into his mother Sarah's tent, and she became his wife and he loved her."

You see, the matchmakers of old were not so concerned about how you fall in love; their concern was whether you *grow* in love. Falling in love is romance, growing in love leads to happy marriage.

And that's true even today. No matter how you fall in love these days, *what is important is not falling in love but growing in love.*

Now I don't suppose we can change the courtship patterns of our youngsters. I rather imagine this is beyond our control. But perhaps we can change their attitudes a little and make this romantic courtship period a kind of testing of the heart in meeting others and in recognizing what is really valuable in a person beyond charm and glamour. Maybe when our sons or daughters say to us, "Mother and Dad, how will I know when I'm in love?" we ought to say more than what we now say, "You'll know, you'll know." We ought to add something else because what we say they'll "know" is largely infatuation.

But there are other things they ought to know, to test that romance, to know if it be true love.

The four ingredients of real love

What would it include? It certainly would include empathy, the feeling of a man and a woman who understand each other so that they don't guard their tongues or hide anything, so that they can speak out their hearts and be themselves. Empathy: a feeling that one heart and the other beat together, a congeniality and fellowship within.

And then the second quality of true love would be concern, concern not that I win her for my wife, but concern that she be happy, my wife or not. Concern that the loved one have the greatest, the finest, the loveliest opportunities for growth and development and happiness.

And third, a pleasure in helping. So many "do" for their wives and "do" for their husbands, but they do it grudgingly: "I've got to do it, so here's my paycheck." When we really love, it's a service of love to give without thought of return.

Then along with this empathy and concern and unselfishness, probably the most important of all is *respect and acceptance*. To respect a person as he is and to accept him as he is because you love him.

Again, an illustration from Jewish family life. On a Friday night, after the candles were lit, and the bread and wine blessed and shared, a Jewish husband would read a love poem to his wife, a Biblical love poem. Now where in the Bible do you suppose he would go for a love poem? The Song of Songs immediately recommends itself, doesn't it? It is some of the most sensual and romantic love poetry ever written. It has to do with beautiful foreheads and lovely skin and white gleaming teeth and lovely black tresses and curves (all the things the advertisements tell you are important in getting a man). But that's *not* the poem a Jewish husband reads on a Friday night. He reads Proverbs, Chapter 31: "A woman of valor who shall find? The heart of her husband doth safely trust in her. He has no lack of gain. She doeth him good and not evil all the days of her life. Many daughters have done valiantly, but thou excellest them all." And then as though to cap the climax and hammer home the message: "Beauty is vain, grace deceitful, but a woman that has reverence for God, she shall be praised."

The secure and stable home must be built on a deep and growing love.

3

Starting Too Soon

A second weakness of the modern family is a social environment that leads to immature marriage and premature divorce. The American family is in trouble because American courtship and marriage are entered too soon, and ended too soon. We are too quick to propose and too quick to dispose.

I believe the major reason for this is the fact that we are raising our youngsters in a hothouse.

In the normal order of things, flowers bloom in the spring, depending on the climate and on the flower, sometime in April, May, or June. But if you want to have flowers earlier in the year, then you put them in a hothouse and force them. With such forcing you can have lovely blossoms in March or even February. But a nurseryman can tell you that hothouse plants which have been forced to early blooming do not do very well when they are transplanted out of doors. They are not very hardy and if they live, it takes them some time to recover from the hothouse treatment.

This is what has happened to our younger generation. They are permitted to get started in the whole routine of courtship too soon. They become forced blooms, lovely to look at, but without much staying power for the time when they are transplanted into homes of their own.

The record of this hothouse growth is plain for anyone to see. Our children go to dancing classes before they are out of grade school. In junior high, they go to dance after dance, and at the dances the lights must be turned low, or the complaints are turned high. By the age of fourteen (in Texas, the law permits driving at this age) they are ready for car dates, which means no parents around to spoil everything. And they begin going steady. They begin going steady before they even begin going. A little girl came home from the fifth grade and said, "Mother, you know I'm going steady with Johnny. He sits near me."

"Well, where are you going dear?"

"Why, we're not going any place. We're just going steady."

From a fifth grader this sounds "cute." But it is actually a warning bell of the kind of hothouse society in which these youngsters are growing up. We see couples who are not old enough to study algebra sitting like old married people at parties—they talk just to each other, they dance just with each other, they walk just with each other. They're cut off from the normal world of childhood.

They marry too soon

And then, of course, if they start dating too soon and going steady too soon, they marry too soon. After all, why not? If a girl's been going out since she's thirteen, by the time she's seventeen she's jaded. She's gone to every kind of party you can give, she's worn every kind of dress that people wear, she's received every kind of corsage that girls receive, and there's nothing left except to settle down. At a time when most girls "in the old days" were coming out for their first date, these girls settle down for their last date.

And if a couple have been going steady for three years when they are seventeen, how long can you go steady?

And when other girls see their friends wearing rings and being showered, and the attractive boys being "snatched up," what is more natural than to want to "get into the act"? And so it's become customary, if you aren't already committed before you leave for college, to spend the freshman year getting the degree of M.R.S.

Or, if a steady romance of several years suddenly breaks up, then it happens frequently that the girl, or sometimes the boy, both still hothouse blooms, have to "show" the other and marry on the rebound just to prove something. (What they usually prove is that to marry on the rebound is a pretty poor foundation for a life partnership.)

And they come to marriage very poorly prepared for life together. Transplanted from a hothouse of premature blooming, they have very little staying power. The evidence for this is in the fact that there are four times as many divorces among those who have married before the age of eighteen as among those who have waited till later. There is a certain maturing process that comes with age and experience, and it cannot be forced. Like almost every other skill men learn, experience is the seasoning teacher. Any expert in the field of driving, for example, can tell you that even though youngsters may have far quicker reaction times than older people, and better eyes for distance and depth, they do not have the judgment that comes with experience. This can come only in time. So can any doctor tell you that to practice medicine requires not only the reading of books and the passing of exams, but endless hours of clinical experience to learn to sense almost by intuition what does not appear to the inexperienced eye.

They divorce too soon

Our youngsters, raised in hothouses, are not prepared to face the realities of marriage. Immature, self-centered, hothouse-forced, everything too soon, now they seek a divorce, and that, too, too soon.

And this is a real problem, too early divorce. Judaism has always permitted divorce. In simple recognition of the fact that some couples just cannot get along no matter how hard they try, Judaism established divorce as a last resort. Today, unfortunately, divorce is frequently a first resort. So many couples, who ought first to be consulting doctors, or counselors, or social workers, or rabbis, go running to the lawyer.

Again, the hothouse technique—trying to force an early bloom of the really delicate flower of marital comradeship, unwilling to go through the sometimes long and patient and difficult task of reconciling two temperaments and two personalities and two value systems until they become, in the words of the Bible, one flesh.

But not only are our young people growing up in a hothouse, the temperature of that hothouse has been raised to feverish pitch by the sex-centered character of our whole environment and the breakdown in the traditional standards of morality. On the one hand, our books and movies and even television programs resemble a prolonged strip tease, all of it whetting the appetite, and on the other hand, more and more voices are lifted suggesting there's little or nothing wrong in satisfying that appetite.

There was a time, a generation ago, when our society held to a double standard. Boys were expected to sow their wild oats; girls to be chaste and pure. With the rise of the feminist movement, the cry arose for a single standard, but the wrong one! Not the single standard of purity that Jews have maintained so zealously for so long, but a single standard of lax and loose behavior.

And Mr. Kinsey, in his research, has revealed in statistics what this has come to mean. But he has not stopped here. Not only has he described the extent to which human behavior has departed from traditional morals, he has suggested that since this is so, we really ought to revise our morals! And, of course, like all ideas and suggestions, this one too has borne fruit, fruit that may satisfy the appetite but poisons the home. All the theory and statistics in the world cannot change the hurt of the human heart when a husband or a wife is unfaithful.

We are raising our youngsters in a hothouse made hotter by our society's tolerance of immorality. Too soon into courtship, too soon into marriage, too soon into divorce courts.

The customs ought to be changed

Is there anything we can do about it? Of course there is, whether we be parents now or young people on the verge of or already married, there are things we can do.

First of all, we who are parents can effect changes in the patterns of the early teens. I said that our children are permitted to get into the courtship phase too soon, but I think a better term might be "encouraged." For who is it that organizes the sixth-grade dancing class? We parents. And who is it that says, when they are going steady, "Aren't they cute?" And who is it that yields to the pressure for car dates? After all, we are their parents. We do not let our youngsters decide whether to go to the dentist to have their teeth cleaned or filled. We take them. We do not let our children decide whether to have a wart removed, we take them. Shall we let them decide when it's time to learn to dance, to give a dance, to have a car date, to go steady? And if they shriek (and believe me they do) we have to remember that "being a parent is not a popularity contest." A group of parents in Dallas whose youngsters were all in the same crowd once organized to keep their children growing in a normal rather than a hothouse way. They called themselves very appropriately "The Stinkers" because to their children, that's what they were. But they stuck to their guns and let their children mature properly.

And believe me, not only is our hothouse method wrong, but our youngsters themselves soon know it. Two or three years ago, a group of young people aged fifteen and sixteen, gathered to develop a youth code for Houston somewhat along the lines of the Minneapolis youth code that made the papers so favorably a few years ago. I was astonished and delighted to discover that fifteen- and sixteen-year-old boys and girls said, "We started going out too soon, and the rules ought to be changed."

There are so many other things for youngsters to do. There's plenty of co-education all day long at school. It doesn't have to be dances and parties. There's skating and bowling and hiking and swimming, there are so many ways to enjoy themselves with other boys, with other girls, even with mixed parties. Let children grow up naturally as children. And this is a parent's obligation, hard as it may be.

Young people in high school and college need some help in avoiding what is a dangerous tendency to start going steady too soon. Now the purpose of modern courtship as distinguished from the arranged matches of several generations ago is to give young people freedom of choice. In courtship days we meet each other and learn to distinguish the superficial from the genuine, the importance of a beautiful heart over a beautiful figure, the importance of getting along with people, and then we winnow out the chaff and find the grain. To start going steady with the first, or second, or third date we have is to cut ourselves off from the freedom of choice that courtship is supposed to provide.

I cannot tell you how many young women and young men have said when I ask them how they ever happened to get married with so much difference between them, "Well, how did I know? We started going steady when I was in the eighth grade. I didn't know but that all boys were like this." And how would one know?

During these courtship years there could be and there ought to be some education of what marriage means, its obligations and its privileges, its duties and its responsibilities. We don't let a child get at the wheel of a car without a course in traffic safety. We don't let a couple get a marriage license without a health examination. Why should we let people who are going to establish a home, a basic unit in society, marry without studying at least the simplest rudiments of getting along, solving quarrels, handling finances—those things upon which many a marriage flounders for lack of experience?

Divorce isn't a solution

Young married couples need to realize one further thing, that *divorce is not the only solution to a troubled marriage*. It's a dissolution; it's a way of saying, "We're not going to solve our problems, we don't even want to try."

Now through the years I have seen some divorces that resulted from completely impossible marriages that should never have taken place, but most of the breakups that I have seen (and I am borne out by the experience of many a marriage counselor and many a minister) could have been avoided if both parties, both husband and wife (*and it takes both*), had been determined to make it work. Some of you can bear testimony to couples who fought their way through five and ten years of miserable married life and emerged from it with fine relationships and relatively happy, serene homes. It's been done. After all, we work at our work. A man reads technical magazines, goes to meetings, consults lawyers, consults accountants to improve his skill. Shall we not work at our home life? A person accepts the ups and downs of finances. This year we make money and next year we lose it. This day is good and the next day is bad. There are ups and downs in marriage, too. There are moments of boredom, there are moments of quarrels, there are moments of love. All are part of it. Divorce does not solve the problems of a marriage. As a matter of fact, the person who is unwilling to work at making a go of marriage and takes the first divorce court out will not be able to give to the next marriage any more than he gave to the first. And the statistics all bear this out.

Marriage is not just a honeymoon. It's a partnership, and it takes thought and intelligence and discipline as well as romance and love.

Perhaps our problem has been, looking at it from another point of view, that we put so high a value on personal happiness that we have been misled into the delusion that a person can be personally happy. It's simply not possible. Personal happiness is built upon personal relationships—to a wife, to a husband, to children, to parents, to associates, to God. And when the relationships are bad then happiness is gone. Happiness is not an apple you pluck off a tree and if you don't like it, pull down another.

Happiness is built on relationships that are basic, sound. This is why the Talmud once said, speaking of marriage, "A man without a wife has no joy, has no cheer, has no hope, in fact he has no life." Personal happiness is found, first of all, in a home, in the achievement of satisfying relationships between a husband and a wife.

4

Husband and Wife:
How Little Time for Loving

A very wise man has said that matches are made in heaven, but marriages are made on earth.

Who, having fallen in love, does not feel that a miracle has taken place? A couple meet under the most wildly improbable circumstances. Young men and women are thrown together in great throngs, and suddenly the eyes of one couple find each other and recognition takes place. Who can account for the wonderful miracle of love?

The rabbis of the Talmud gave God the credit. When a curious Roman matron asked what God had been doing since He had divided the Red Sea, they replied that He had been busy at matchmaking. "That's silly," she replied. "Who needs God for this? I can make matches." And she bought a thousand slaves, half male and half female, and matched them up. But to her dismay, none of them liked each other—she had failed to reckon with the mystery of love. After this experience she agreed with the rabbis. God must make the match.

But although God makes matches, marriages are made on earth; marriages are made successful by husbands and wives who know they cannot rely on primary attraction alone. Love is the mood of a match, but without mutual respect and mutual understanding and mutual forbearance, God's matchmaking will fail.

God can make a match, but men and women can unmake a marriage, because love alone is not enough. Marriage is built on a foundation of love, but without walls and a roof it cannot survive life's storms. Marriage includes a sense of responsibility, a devotion to duty, a shared understanding of what is important, a clear agreement on money matters, a common religious outlook.

Even as a God-given talent can go to waste if it is not trained, disciplined, organized, and directed, so the love that is a couple's gift from God will wither away if they do not work at their home life.

Matches are made by God; marriages are made on earth.

One way they are made successful is by sharing one hundred per cent.

Don't bog down in bookkeeping

Every once in a while, in counseling with young lovers who are planning a wedding and a wedded life, I hear a young voice say with such cocky assurance, "Marriage is give-and-take; it's a fifty-fifty proposition." But whenever I hear those words, I wince a little because what seems good logic is bad "psychologic." A marriage built on the idea of fifty-fifty is almost sure to falter because it involves too much bookkeeping. People who think along these lines tend to calculate whether they are getting their share. "If I gave in yesterday, then you must give in today." "If you get your way today, then I must get my way tomorrow."

Marriage cannot be built on a fifty-fifty partnership. If both a husband and wife want to have a truly successful marriage, they must be more anxious to give than to get, more anxious to please than to be pleased. And if proportions must be stated, they should be one hundred-one hundred.

The Bible says this in the curious way in which it speaks of the creation of the human race. In Genesis' first chapter, we read: "Male and female He created them and He called *their name Adam*." It is almost as though to say that a man or

woman is not quite complete alone, that marriage is the ful-
fillment of self; therefore, a man and woman are not fifty-
fifty partners, but one hundred per cent partners, "and they
shall become one flesh."

That marriage begins best, therefore, in which a man says
to a woman, "I love you and I want *you* to be happy," and in
which at the same time she says, "I want *you* to be happy."
Then, not through any mechanical formula of fifty-fifty, but
in one hundred per cent concern for each other, they will
create a happy home.

Homes can be broken by many things. Divorces can be
caused by adultery, alcoholism, and apathy. Husbands and
wives separate because of arguments over money, over in-
laws, over social friends. But I am beginning to suspect that
many a marriage comes to an end because neither a husband
nor a wife can bear to be wrong in a discussion, and, what is
worse, each is overbearing when proved in the right.

This thought was provoked by hearing the casual remark of
a sociologist who said that statistics showed there were more
divorces in an election year than at other times. I could not
believe it at first, but then my mind went back to the kinds of
quarrels that people have told me of, and suddenly I realized
that for elections to cause divorces was perfectly true to life.

There are people who just cannot bear to be wrong, and
there are people who delight in proving themselves right, and
when two of these get together, the temperature goes up. A
husband makes a simple remark about the big snow ten years
ago. "Oh no, it was eleven," replies his wife, and off they go!
But she *must* prove she is right and gets out the almanac.
"There, you see," she cries triumphantly, "it was eleven years
ago." "No," shouts the husband, "that's not the storm I was
talking about."

Familiar? Yet it is just such foolish arguments which can
undermine a home. This is why there are more divorces in
election years.

The message seems plain. If you want a happy home, then

admit it when you are wrong. But even more, if you are right, do not insist on proving it. "It is far better," in the charming words of Edmond Cahn, professor of law at New York University, "to establish a home than an opinion."

Love transforms all of life

The miracle of love is its ability to transform all of life. Through the years I have stood in wonder as one bride and groom after another have looked into each other's eyes and mutually promised a lifetime of loyalty and devotion. And I never cease to be amazed at the miracle that love does achieve.

For love transforms the whole of life. Every bride is beautiful, you know. Some are more beautiful than others, but none is less than beautiful. Not only to her groom, but to all who see her. Love transforms the ordinary and the plain into the beautiful.

Love transforms the tasks of life. That which we would not do for money or fame, we will do for love. For look you—how many people would deliberately seek a job as dishwasher, how many people would apply for a job as diaper launderer? We will take such jobs if we are hungry and this is all there is available. But seek such jobs? Yet every woman who loves a man will wash dishes and launder diapers and sing while she does it.

Love transforms the heart of a man. For man has a wanderlust—he loves his freedom, to come and to go, to take to the trail, to search the far horizon. And for love he settles down and builds a nest, and happily surrenders his freedom to the woman he loves and the children their love brings them.

Love transforms a home. All of us know from experience. Let a husband and a wife quarrel, the house is still there and the furniture and the meals on time, but where is the home?

Love transforms the children. Every experiment, physical and psychological, proves it again and again. Children who are unloved, children raised in homes without love, are physically, mentally, and psychologically crippled.

Love transforms all of life.

These thoughts came to my mind as I watched the wedding waltz. The ceremonies were over, the cake had been cut, and now the young couple were dancing—for the moment the only couple on the floor. Beautiful! Young, lovely to look at, with heaven in their eyes.

But suddenly, as I sat there, my heart smote me. I began to think of all the heartaches, pain, and tears that were in store for young couples. Who knows what misery, what evil fortunes, what tragedy may overtake them?

Even in the normal course of life, there are tears enough, and who is lucky enough to be normal? There are miscarriages, and babies born only to die. There are financial reverses and the bitter misery of poverty. There are the problems of growing children and the growing problems of troubled children. There are operations and accidents and the sad shake of a doctor's head.

These are all the things that "life" can do to a couple. Then there are the things they do to each other. Marriages can turn bitter; the sweetness of the wedding waltz can sour to vinegar. Happiness can be destroyed by intolerance, when neither can accept the other as he is but seek vainly to strait-jacket a partner into a mirror of oneself. It can be wrecked by disloyalty—not only physical unfaithfulness, but the kind of unfaithfulness that ignores and shows contempt. It can be soured by nagging, by stinginess, by holding grudges, by losing tempers. Yes, my heart smote me as I watched them dance, so young, so beautiful, so unaware.

But then as the family joined the newlyweds on the floor, I saw a white-haired couple dance in stately one-two-three across the floor. They were the bride's grandparents. They, too, were beautiful to look upon—serene and happy faces, revealing the shared love and companionship of the years. They had faced all the dangers and all the fates, endured the headaches and heartaches. Theirs was the harvest of love.

It can be done, I thought, and looked again at the young couple no longer full of foreboding. You will shed tears. Who does not? But with love you will dry them. So dance, and be happy; love and be blessed.

A prayer for the young

There is another beautiful lesson for family life in one of Walter Rauschenbusch's profound prayers: ". . . and love our loved ones with an added tenderness, because the days of love are short."

This would seem at first glance to be a prayer for the twilight years when we have so little time left, but the aging do not need to be reminded. It is the young who need this prayer, because time does fly by so quickly. Our children grow up overnight and move away to make their own homes; our spouses age, disease and death snatch them from us. The days of love are short.

And yet how little time we give to loving. We have time to spend on so many things. We work overtime at our job, our profession, our business. We have time to squander on so many things, hobbies, play. Yes, we have time to give to everything.

But, as a colleague of mine points out, we are misers of the time we spend with our families. We dole it out in tiny bits. The wife suggests spending an evening sitting before the fire; the lad says, "Dad, let's play some ball"; the daughter suggests that we eat outside. But we haven't time, or we do not want to find time. We're tired from a day's work or a day's play, we haven't time for the added tenderness. We forget that the days of love are short.

Later we remember. We sigh over days that are gone forever; we ask where has the time all gone. I suspect this is the reason grandparents give so much of themselves to grandchildren. It is not only the joy of the occasion, but more, they realize how little time they spent with their own children and are resolved to spend more with their grandchildren. The days of love are short.

And when life is spent and all added up, what are the memories that warm our hearts? The happy laughter of a child as we swung him high; the joys of an after-dinner hour when we put aside the dishwashing for a bit and just sat and talked; the movie we saw together and the ice cream we enjoyed after it; the walk through the woods and sharing the lore of wildlife. The days of love are short, but oh, so rich!

5

Parents and Children: Challenge to Love

"Mother's Day is a hoax and a fraud," said the Cynic.

"Why?" I asked.

"Because it's all public display," the Cynic replied. "It just encourages lip service and showiness, but it does not mean a thing. I know a mother who sits lonely and neglected all year long. Then, on Mother's Day, her son sends her a great big bouquet of roses, so that everybody will say, 'What a wonderful son you have. Look at that bouquet!' Mother's Day is a hoax."

"Now wait a minute," I interrupted. "If there were *no* Mother's Day, she might not even get that yearly bouquet. I agree with you that it would be much better if children would honor their parents and show their love by their daily words and deeds, but even a once-a-year reminder is better than none.

"Who knows but that this Mother's Day some son, in the act of buying his yearly bouquet, will suddenly be conscience-smitten about his neglect till this moment and begin again to show each day his loyalty and love? Who knows? Mother's Day is not her only day, but sometimes we need Mother's Day to remind us that this is so."

The Bible, as we already know, describes the ideal wife and mother in Proverbs, Chapter 31: "A woman of valor, who shall find? For her price is far above rubies."

The poem goes on to detail her worth, to describe how

diligent she was, how well she looked to the ways of her household. She fed them and clothed them and did not eat the bread of idleness. She worked willingly with her hands, buying a field and planting a vineyard, seeking wool and flax, holding the spindle and distaff, and making linen garments.

In some ways the words have a quaint and antique sound. Our modern mothers no longer "clothe their households in scarlet" (do you suppose this was red woolen underwear?) nor deliver girdles to the merchant (it's the other way around!). But they are just as busy, just as industrious, in looking well to the ways of the modern household. They bring our food from afar, from supermarkets instead of village markets; they drive their husbands and children in motor pools to work, to school, to music lessons, to religious school. They may no longer weave their own cloth, but busy themselves with many another do-it-yourself project. They give food to their households, help the children with homework, and stretch out their hand to the poor by going to meetings of modern charities, and take part in mothers' drives on polio.

The same praise was offered in a single word on a mortician's record.

Mother as the homemaker

I was once called to officiate at the funeral of a remarkable woman I had known for as long as I have been in Texas. She and her husband had a happy life together for more than fifty years; their children are an ornament to the communities in which they live.

From among my many memories, I had begun to compose a fitting eulogy, when at the funeral home I happened to glance at the minister's little record card which the mortician handed me. Such cards include the name, address, age, and so forth of the deceased, and on this card there was a space for occupation. In that space, where one would normally expect the usual word "housewife," the mortician had written "homemaker." And when my eyes lighted on that, I knew what I would say at this gracious lady's funeral service, for she was truly not just a housewife but a homemaker.

A housewife, as Webster's dictionary suggests, is the female head of the household, but a homemaker—ah, that's something much more. A housewife keeps house, but a homemaker builds a home. A housewife suggests skill, efficiency, cleanliness, economy, but a homemaker suggests warmth, affection, sweetness, and goodness.

Mothers may be housewives (houses have to be kept) but most of all they are homemakers, filling their homes with love.

"I want to be like Daddy!"

Mothers are the source of love; fathers, on the other hand, provide their children with a model. Nothing pleases a father more than to hear his son say, "Daddy, when I grow up I want to be just like you!" This is the ultimate compliment of affection; it is the highest praise a child can give to his father.

But tell me, fellow fathers, do you feel the same way? Do you want your son to be just like you? Would you be satisfied if he grew up to be what you are, talk as you talk, act as you act? Are you the kind of man you want your son to be?

When he says to you, "Daddy, I want to be just like you," he is telling you that you are a fine father. But are you the kind of man you want your son to be?

This matter was brought home to me not long ago by a young man I met in the hospital. His wife had just given birth to their first baby, a son, and instead of being, like the usual father, wild with joy, this young man said to me, "Rabbi, I feel an almost terrifying sense of responsibility. I will be the man in this boy's life, almost the only man in his life until he is old enough to join the Boy Scouts. Am I the kind of man a boy should have in his life?"

When children imitate their parents, everyone laughs. There is something very charming about the little boy who swaggers like his dad, or the little girl who puts on her mother's high-heeled shoes. But sometimes that laughter turns into tears. For in much deeper ways children imitate their parents as long as they live, and what parents do is in turn done to them.

I remember a story which tears at the heart. There was a home in which a lone grandfather lived with his son, his son's wife, and their little boy. The old man was getting a little feeble and when he ate, the food sometimes spilled from his trembling hands or dribbled from his mouth. The daughter-in-law could not stand the sight of this, and insisted that the grandfather be put in the kitchen by himself at mealtime and his food placed in a large wooden bowl to prevent his spilling it on the table or on the floor.

Some weeks passed. One day the little grandson was busy in the yard whittling away at a large chunk of wood. "What are you making, son?" his father asked. The answer shook him. "I'm carving a bowl for you to eat out of when you get old."

Does it seem far-fetched? The newspapers once reported that a father and his eighteen-year-old son were arrested for bank robbery. There was a son who was following in his father's footsteps!

But the converse is also true. Children also follow what they see of sweetness and consideration. The mother of a five-year-old was expecting another baby. The little boy did not quite understand why, but he noticed that his father was quite solicitous of his mother's safety, helping her up and down stairs and so forth. When his father was out of the city for a couple of days, the son, seeing his mother about to descend the stairs, called, "Wait! Let me help you like Daddy does."

Family counselors say that the best way to have a happy home when you marry is to come from one. The implications of this are plain. Do you want your children to have a high character, a good life? Then develop a high character. Do you want your children to have a happy married life? Give them a happy marriage to imitate. What children see, they do. What parents do is in turn done to them.

We can learn something about good parenthood from the results of failure. Three young men who had been in trouble, and who had served time in the Training School for Boys in Eldora, Iowa, were asked by the editor of the school newspaper to tell what they would do for and with their children *if they were parents*. And this is what they wrote:

The first lad suggested: "I would make sure my children had good religious training and background. I would take time out to do the things they wanted to do and I would be interested in those things which were of interest to them. I'd try to understand their problems, too. A person should always treat his children in a manner which will make them feel wanted."

From a second came these words: "I would teach them to respect their parents and to obey us when we give a command. They would learn how to become members of a happy family group working together."

"I would first teach them to have proper respect for the law and for the people who enforce it," wrote another. "Secondly, I would teach them always to tell the truth, even though it may hurt at times. Stealing may start out small, but it always ends up big."

These are wise words under any circumstances, but when you know who wrote them, your heart could break as you read what they say. In a way, between the lines, they are crying out to their mothers and fathers, "Why didn't you stop us before it was too late?"

And out of their wise words, and the situation in which those words were spoken, there comes a challenge to all of us, a challenge to give our children a sense of being loved, a sense of right and wrong, and a respect for the right and those who enforce it. Could anyone say it better than these boys?

Parental self-control

In all the current talk about juvenile delinquency, we often lose sight of the fact that parents' biggest problem is not controlling their children, but controlling themselves. If we, as parents, are hot-tempered or weak-willed, irritable or complacent, impatient or shortsighted, then, before we begin to complain of our teen-agers' lack of self-discipline, we need to learn self-control for ourselves.

Item: a cartoon in which a father, face red and hair on end, comes stomping back into the room with these words: "I'll teach *him* to lose his temper. I broke every car of his toy train!"

Item: a child in a restaurant set up such a howl at a mother's *no* that in weak surrender she reversed herself and said *yes*. (How in the name of Heaven is that child ever to learn to say *no* to himself?)

Item: a question that should be asked, "If nagging a spouse leads to a broken home, why should we assume that daily nagging of a child will lead to a fine character?"

Item: all this youngster wanted was to be like everyone else, wear the same clothes and hair-do, read the same comics, hum the same tunes. This is typical of adolescence. But the mother could not stand it; her daughter must not be a sheep. On the other hand, a father sat complacently while being told of some really vicious escapades of his son, and said: "Oh, he'll grow out of it; I was the same way when I was his age."

Item: parents are indulgent one day and strict the next, laugh at some fresh remark on Tuesday and slap the child's face for the same remark on Wednesday. Such parents are training their children by moods rather than rules, and their inconsistency leads to worry and uncertainty in children.

Parents have moods, but they must control them in the treatment of their children.

The biggest asset in controlling children is self-control in parents.

The family-centered family

Sociologists frequently describe the family by its center of authority. There is the patriarchal in which the father dominates; the matriarchal in which the mother wears the trousers; recently we have seen the development of the child-centered family in which everything revolves about the little ones. But the best family, it seems to me, is the family-centered family in which there is an emphasis on every member of the family, in which each has his role to play and his load to carry. It was such a family that developed in Jewish history and which the sociologist Bess Cunningham described thirty years ago as perhaps the most important contribution of the Jew to modern life.

In that family, husband and wife were mutually obligated to each other in love and loyalty; parents were obligated to children, and children likewise to parents, and over it all presided the "peace of the house" which made for mutual interdependence and family solidarity.

This family has stood the test of time. Its character is a model for an age that needs desperately to recover the strength of its family life.

For the stakes are high. Long ago, the prophet Malachi, in foretelling the coming of the Kingdom, said that before that day Elijah will come and turn the hearts of children to parents and the hearts of parents to children and *then* will come the day of the Lord. The implication is plain. In trying to build a better world, we must begin with a better family.

IV

Living with Your Neighbors

1

Trade Lovingly

To live with our neighbors requires the unselfish love of neighbors.

I heard a very interesting conversation one day.

"People are just naturally selfish," said one.

"Then why are they constantly hurting themselves?" asked the other. "If they are so selfish, why do they do things that bring them trouble? Selfishness begets misery; unselfishness brings happiness. Maybe the best selfishness is unselfishness."

And it reminded me of something Yehudah Steinberg wrote in one of his Hebrew stories. In it, a pious man expresses a naïve astonishment at the stupidity of the wicked. "The main reason," he said, "for doing wicked deeds is the pursuit of pleasure. But what greater pleasure is there than the joy of doing a good deed? If you steal an apple and eat it, you have only the taste of the apple and whatever bad conscience your soul may be capable of. But if you take your own apple and give it to someone who is hungry, you get a thousand times more pleasure—you get the pleasure of seeing him enjoy it, the pleasure of being thanked, and the pleasure of feeling that you have done a really good deed. If only the wicked were smart enough to recognize this, they would abandon their evil ways and all become saints just for the sake of the pleasure it brings."

The simplicity and naïveté of this little story is charming, but it assumes that pleasure is all of one piece. The same assumption is made by the Cynic who, hearing of someone's generous gift to a hospital, sneers, "He only does it because it gives him pleasure. Why should he be praised?"

There is a difference between physical pleasure and mental, there is a difference between sensual enjoyment and spiritual. And to call upon people to come to unselfish action by the way of selfish ambition is to miss that difference by a mile.

Unselfishness is not a higher form of selfishness at all. It is a very deliberate choice of the good of others over our own. It may bring satisfactions, and these should not be begrudged, but the good life is not a search for pleasure as product or by-product; it is a search for goodness and for God.

Such unselfish neighborliness was described in a very striking way by the customer of a small-town merchant whom I buried some years ago. The phrase the customer and friend used was, "He traded so loving." It was an inelegant way of putting it, perhaps, but what an elegant compliment to any man!

All of us believe in love; we all talk about the Golden Rule, but this was a man who lived it, and lived it where it was most difficult, in his business life. Most of us, I suspect, reserve our love for other than business hours. We save it for our home life, for our family. But do we trade loving?

We love our friends, we help our neighbors, we take soup to Mrs. Jones when she is sick, pick up Aunt Susie to take her to religious services. We enjoy our "buddies," golfing with them, helping them build a fence. But business—ah, that's another matter. Too many of us leave our love behind us when we open the door to our office or our store.

Sometimes we put it bluntly: "Dog eat dog." And sometimes we put it humorously: "The Golden Rule of business is to do your neighbor before he does you." How many of us trade loving?

And this applies not only to the seller of goods; it applies to the buyer as well. Listen sometimes to the stories told by clerks of the discourtesy and rudeness and hatefulness customers will show to those who wait on them. And so likewise to all areas of work. The laborer can work loving or hating, the employer can hire loving or hating. One of the worst evils let loose on the world by Marxism was the whole concept of the class struggle—that buyer and seller, owner and renter, employer and worker are and must be economic enemies, that one must triumph over the other and destroy him. Marx would not believe that anyone can trade loving. But they can, and they have.

It takes effort, but the effort is the test of how deeply you really believe in the Bible's demand that we love our neighbor as ourselves.

The first question on Judgment Day

Have you ever wondered about Judgment Day? Have you ever asked yourself: What will it be like in that final courtroom when God sits, as it were, in a courtroom on high, and each of us appears before Him to answer for our lives and the way that we lived them? Have you ever wondered?

What do you suppose are the first questions that He will ask? What will He regard as most important? What do you think?

We would not be the first to wonder about this. There was speculation about it in the Talmud sixteen or seventeen centuries ago. Rabbah, one of the great teachers of his age, said: "When the heavenly court brings a man to trial, the *first question* asked of him will be, '*Were you honest in your business?* In earning your living, did you deal honorably with the man you worked for, the men and women who worked for you, with your clients, your patients, your customers, your competitors, or with the law? Were you an honest man?'"

This question strikes at one of the greatest problems of our time. In private affairs and public, in business and in government, there have been, during the past few years, more corruption, more scandals, more barefaced and brazen robberies than at any other time I can remember, and I can remember Teapot Dome.

Think of them all—local, statewide, nationwide—land sales, insurance, lobbies, labor racketeering, vicuña coats; pilfering, embezzling, stealing. And to top it off, a poll reports that forty per cent of our college students admit openly to cheating, and are not one bit ashamed. And this is worst of all, not to be ashamed. The crime is not what you do, but getting caught at it, and the public yawns indifferently. They don't even care. Some public official is caught with his hand in the cookie jar, and people say, "We don't pay our public officials enough," as though to say it's all right for a man to be dishonest until he can afford to be honest.

Honesty is held in low esteem today, yet without it, an economy fails; without it, governments rot; without it, our way of life is headed for destruction. Honesty is not a matter of personal pride, but a fundamental law of life. Down the centuries, God's voice echoes, "Thou shalt not steal." At the end of time, His question awaits us, "Have you been honest in your business?"

This idea is underlined by another Talmudic comment. The sages read the Biblical story of the Flood and were puzzled. The Bible said the world was full of wickedness. "But what kind of wickedness?" asked the sages. "Were there no courts in those days, no judges, no jails for wrongdoers? What could have been the cause of the flood?" "The world was full of little crimes," said one rabbi. "People stole things of such small value—a toothpick, a twig of firewood, a strawberry—that they could not be prosecuted. Who would arrest a man for so trivial a crime? Yet, the sum total of these tiny wrongs was so staggering as to bring on the Flood."

Dishonesty is wrong any time and all the time. It is wrong in business and on the golf links, wrong in the labor union and on the basketball court, in the classroom and on the television. Dishonesty is wrong.

And you cannot make any exceptions. You cannot say, "I believe in honesty, *but* . . . I believe in telling the truth, *but* . . . Lying is wrong, *but* . . ."

Now this does not mean that you have to be brutal with the truth. Truth can be tactful, but tact must also be truthful. When a lady asks you how you like her hat, you do not have to tell a white lie, or any kind of lie. You can say that the color is becoming, or that it is very stylish, or you can say with enthusiasm, "Now that's what I call a hat!"

Dishonesty is wrong. And little lies are no different in quality than big lies. In fact, little lies lead to big lies. In the quiz show-fixing scandal some years ago, the people accused had just told a small lie. And yet when they were brought before a grand jury, one hundred out of the one hundred fifty did break the law and commit perjury. Little lies lead to big lies.

The same thing applies to classroom cheating. Most of our children are more or less guilty of it, and even when not guilty, do not look down very much on those who are. After all, they point out, who's being cheated? The student who copies is not taking something away from the student whose paper is being copied. The cheater does not rob the better prepared student of anything. He only cheats himself.

But is this so? Is that the only one who is cheated?

Suppose your life were at stake and you put its fate in the hands of a doctor who had cheated the day your condition was being studied? Suppose your freedom were at stake and your defense was in the hands of a lawyer who had relied on a crib to pass exams? Little lies lead to large evils.

After all, our whole society, our whole civilization is built on mutual faith and mutual trust. If I cannot trust you and you cannot trust me, if every man's hand is in another man's pocket, if every man takes every opportunity to chisel, what chance do we have?

We get into an airplane. If the engineers who drew the plans were dishonest, if the mechanics who put it together were dishonest, if the pilots who tested it were dishonest, if the airlines and the National Board of Aeronautics were all dishonest, what plane would ever fly?

We eat bread. If the farmer who grew the wheat was dishonest, if the miller who ground the flour was dishonest, if the baker who baked it and the storekeeper who sold it were dishonest, how long would we eat bread? Our world is built, our world must be built, on truthfulness, on honesty.

Now of course we try to protect ourselves. We have laws, we have inspectors, we have boards, we have regulations, we have policemen, but in the long run a law can only codify public morality. A law is the seal of public approval; it only reflects the majority's willingness to abide by it *before* it is passed. A law is not made for the lawful, it is made for the lawless; and if people are not honest, no law can make them honest.

What we need in America today is a private rededication to truth, to integrity, to honesty. For only if each of us is honest in his every dealing with his fellow man can there be public honesty in the relationship of men. If we shrug it it all off with the quiet statement, "There's a little larceny in all of us," then we are resigning ourselves to little evils which one day will become large evils.

A sin against ourselves

Dishonesty, furthermore, is not only a sin against society, it is a sin against ourselves.

Edwin Markham wrote a story-poem about a wealthy man who asked a local carpenter to build a cottage for him. For long hours these two men studied over the plans for the cottage and checked every little detail. It was specified that this home was to be very carefully built with only the very finest materials. The workmanship was to be of the best. The carpenter was urged, "Don't worry about time or expense. Work carefully, slowly, and do the best possible job."

Then, when the job was about ready to begin, when the plans had all been made, and the house about to be built, the wealthy man told the carpenter that he was leaving town and would not be back for a year, but felt sure that by the time he returned the house would be finished.

Now the carpenter had always been a trusted employee. He was a man who had taken pride in his work, but when his employer left the city for a whole year, he began to think about the opportunity this gave him to make a little extra money. He didn't have to use the best lumber—by the time the man came back it would be covered with paint and no one would know the difference. In the plumbing, he didn't have to use the best pipes. Soon the pipes would be covered with wallboard, and not be seen. So, too, with the finishing— it did not have to be done so carefully. So the carpenter built the house as cheaply and as shoddily as he thought he could, saying to himself, "The owner will never know the difference."

A year passed, and the wealthy man returned from his long trip. And he didn't know the difference at all. He didn't even look to see because he had learned through the years to trust this carpenter's integrity and his expert ability. And so, with just a fleeting look at the house, he said, "You have always been a man I could trust, and now I want to give you a present to show how much I appreciate you. I had in mind, when we planned this house, to give it to you. It is yours. Take it."

And this is the way it is all the time in life. Everything we do, ultimately we do for or to ourselves. But how we cherish the fond delusion that this is not so! The doctor puts us on a diet (whether for some disorder or to keep our weight down) and we take some forbidden fruit surreptitiously and say, "I'll just cheat my diet a little." Whom are we cheating? The house of our bodies is ours, and if we cheat, we cheat ourselves.

We go into business or a profession and there are so many ways to scamp. You can sweep the dirt under the rug, cut corners here and there. It's easily done, but whom are we scamping in the long run? No one but ourselves.

It's our house, this body of ours, this mind, this soul, and if we build it with shoddy materials and put it together with shoddy workmanship, then we've got to live in it till the day we die. And if it is cheap and flimsy and badly put together, it's we and we alone who are miserably housed.

Our trouble is that we don't look ahead. Temporarily, shoddy work can look good. Temporarily it looks like a fine house. But poor workmanship always shows up in the long run (come the rains, and the wind, and the cold, and then you know what sort of house you live in). So let us build our hearts' houses with care, with devotion, with the best of materials and the finest of workmanship, for it is our house, the dwelling of our soul forever.

2

Who Is Thy Neighbor?

Speaking of neighborly love, who *is* our neighbor?

Judaism faced this question a long time ago. In a Talmudic classroom, the teacher asked his students, "What is the most important verse in the Bible?" A hand shot up, a voice cried out, "Leviticus, Chapter nineteen, verse eighteen. 'Thou shalt love thy neighbor as thyself.'"

Then another hand was raised, and another voice, "But Rabbi, who is thy neighbor?"

A good question, isn't it? A very good question. Who is our neighbor? Because after all, everyone believes in loving his neighbor. This is not just Judaism, it is Christianity, Buddhism, Mohammedanism, and Confucianism. Hitler taught men to love their neighbors, that is, if their neighbors were Aryan, were Fascist, were German. Communism has a consuming love of man as long as that man is not a bourgeois, not a capitalist, as long as he is a member of the Communist Party, or at least, docile to its leadership. Malan of South Africa preaches a love of neighbors, if they are white in color, and Dutch Reformed in religion, and Afrikaans in language. Who does not believe in loving his neighbor?

Yes, it was a good question, a very good question: Who is our neighbor? Just those who live next door? Just those who live in our town? Just those who are our color, or go to our church, or belong to our political party? Who is our neighbor?

"What then," asked the rabbi, "would *you* say is the most important verse in the Bible?" And the student then answered, "To me, the most important verse in the Bible is in Genesis: 'In the image of God He created man.' Because it is this verse which tells us who our neighbor is."

All men are neighbors, because all men are created in God's image.

There are several interesting Talmudic commentaries upon that verse which emphasize this truth. One of them tells that when God was ready to create man, He took a bit of earth from each continent and a bit of water from every lake and with this clay made man, so that no people might claim: "This is where man was created; we who live here are, therefore, of finer stock."

Another commentator noted that whereas animals and birds and crawling things seem to have been created in large numbers, Adam was the one and only man created from the beginning. Why should God have created but one man? To make it impossible for any man to consider himself superior to another by virtue of ancestry. For all men are descended from one man, and no man may say, "My family is better than yours, my family tree is older." We are all descended from great-great-grandpa Adam.

Another rabbi of old made man's creation in God's image the source of man's right to be different. "Look at the contrast," he said, "between an earthly king and the King of the Universe. A monarch issues coins upon which he stamps his image, profile or full-face, and no matter how many coins he issues, they are all alike. But when the King of the Universe stamps His image upon men, millions of them, no two are exactly alike." God made us different; it is our divine right.

This is precisely where democracies and totalitarianisms differ. Tyrants of the left or right wipe out all who persist in differing, so that their subjects begin to look like coins, talking alike, voting alike, even thinking alike. Democracy, on the other hand, protects man's right to differ, even encourages individualism.

In Nazi Germany, dissenters were sent to the concentration camps; in Communist China, they are brainwashed; in America, they go to the ballot box, and if they are outvoted, they wait four years and try again!

The first chapter of Genesis has thus left its stamp upon our lives, our ethics, our politics. It makes all men neighbors, and the love of neighbor must therefore include all men.

Prejudice is poison

The opposite of good will is prejudice.

Prejudice is the hatred of neighbors without cause. It is rather like poison ivy. The poison is not on the person who touches the ivy, but in the ivy. Let me illustrate.

We often feel ill-treated by others. We buy a dress that does not fit, a workman does a poor job, or someone fails to pay what he owes us. Just contrast our reaction in such situations when the person we think has done us ill is a member of our own church, and when he is a member of some other religious (or racial) group. In the first instance, we criticize the individual. *He* is dishonest, *he* is inefficient, *he* is a cheat. But in the second instance, when he is of another faith, how often do we say, "Just like a —— [supply your own]." We no longer think of him as an individual, we think of him as belonging to a group. The prejudice was there already, just like poison on ivy. What he did was to brush against it.

This same truth can be seen from another angle. We meet and get to know and to admire someone from a group we dislike. What do we say? Do we say, "I was wrong about the group." Not if we are prejudiced. If we are prejudiced, we say, "I don't like —— [supply your own again] but you're different." Again we reveal the true character of prejudice. What we imply by such a statement is this: "I don't like your people, and I am not going to let your good qualities disturb my prejudice. I am going to like you and still dislike them."

Prejudice *is* a poison, and in addition it is completely irrational. Its unreasoning blindness is perfectly illustrated by a true story.

The story was related by a mother about her six-year-old son, Billy. He came into the house one day from play and announced to her, "Donny is silly."

"Why is Donny silly?"

"He just is. Yesterday he said I was his best friend. Today he said he doesn't like me any more. And when I asked him why, he said it was because I am Jewish. Isn't that silly?"

Isn't that silly? And yet what a vivid example of what prejudice really is. Billy was no different that day than he had been the day before; he was the same child with the same good and bad points. But Donny had changed. Donny had been taught to hate a name, a label, a group, and so now he did not like Billy any more.

There have been a number of attempts to analyze the sources of this irrational form of behavior called prejudice.

Some say it is jealousy. Some say that when members of a minority group begin to make good, when they begin to live in nice houses, drive big cars and get their names in the paper, then envy raises its ugly head, and prejudice takes over. But this theory falls down because prejudice is not directed against the successful alone; it is directed against the entire group, whether it be Catholics, Jews, or Baptists.

Some say it is all economics, that minorities are the scapegoats of depressions, and that when men are hungry, they look for someone on whom to vent their frustrations. Once it was the Huguenots; once it was the Irish; once it was the Jews. The favorite legend of this school of thought has to do with an aboriginal tribe in Australia who are said to live on the fruit of the bongo-bongo tree. When the crop is good, the members of the tribe eat the fruit of the bongo-bongo tree, and offer it to strangers. When the crop is only fair, the natives eat, but the strangers go hungry. When the crop fails, then the natives eat the strangers!

And it is true that depressions are a breeding ground for the *antis*—whatever they're *anti*. But this is like saying that disease thrives in a weakened body. The disease is not created by the weakness, only encouraged by it.

Since the fall of Hitler, and the revelations of the enormity of the crimes of Hitlerism not only against six million Jews but many millions of Poles, Cossacks, gypsies, and other national groups the Nazis considered inferior races, the scientists, psychologists, and sociologists have made a study of prejudice, and they have suggested some interesting theories as to its source.

They say that one of the main causes of the mental disorder of prejudice is an attitude we might call authoritarian, an attitude that sees all society structured into levels, into castes, with each person neatly ticketed as to who he is and where on the ladder he stands, and as long as people stay in their place and recognize their position and do not attempt to change it, then all is well, and in the authoritarian mind society is well regulated. But let people begin to move out of the orbit assigned them, and the reaction is passionate. Let minority groups refuse to be the hewers of wood and the drawers of water, let them claim or seek equal rights, let them run for office, achieve great wealth or honor, and then the sick soul of the *anti* erupts in a volcano of prejudice.

And when it does, watch out! For prejudice is a two-edged sword that ultimately destroys not only the irrationally prejudiced but those who let themselves be led and misled by them.

A gallows thirty cubits high

The Biblical story of Esther illustrates this two-edged quality of prejudice. Haman, the authoritarian personality, already prejudiced against the stranger, the minority, the Jews of Persia, the poison in him aroused by the fact that Mordecai, out of religious conviction, refused to bow down to him and thus refused to "keep his place," determined upon the destruction of the Jewish people. And for Mordecai he reserved a special end by building a gallows thirty cubits high. The end of the story—Haman was hanged high on the very gallows he had built for Mordecai, and seventy-five thousand of those who had followed him were slain.

Prejudice is a two-edged sword. In history, prejudice has not only destroyed those who held it but endangered whole nations. We have seen this in our own time, and we ought to have learned our lesson well.

A modern Haman came to the German people thirty years ago and agitated: "There is a certain people . . . and it profiteth not the German nation to suffer them . . . let them be destroyed, and I will add to your coffers . . ." Enough people listened to give Adolph Hitler his chance at power, and with that power he almost destroyed the Jewish people.

But he also destroyed much of the German nation too, the tolerant with the prejudiced, the innocent with the guilty. Their cities were bombed to rubble, their factories reduced to dust. Their young men were slain on the battlefield and their children in bomb shelters. Their nation was defeated in war, and divided in peace so that to this day millions of Hitler's victims, his own people, live under the heel of Communism. In contrast to the story of Esther, not only was Hitler meted out his just reward, not only were his bigoted followers poisoned by their own hearts' hatred, but the whole German people suffered from his prejudice.

We need to understand this clearly. Intolerance is like a poison in the bloodstream, a cancer in the body politic; it is dangerous to our freedom, our democracy. When the panderers of prejudice come to us and play on our dislike of some racial or religious minority, they are not seeking *our* welfare; they are seeking their own power, and with that power they will destroy all of us.

The building of tolerance and brotherhood in our own

hearts and in our society is not, you see, merely the pursuit of a luxury. Brotherhood is not like air conditioning in a car, which makes driving more comfortable; it is like lubrication without which the car cannot run at all for very long.

Prejudice is dangerous to America. Good will is the safeguard of democracy.

Learn to live with good will

How then, can we build good will? Both by attitude and by action.

Let me illustrate the attitude by a parable and the action by a true story.

The parable: I love my mother. I truly believe that she is the most wonderful mother in all the world. And I would not trade mothers with anyone. And yet, while I love my mother dearly and still think that no one else can compare with her, I know that others love their mothers too, and that they too believe their mother to be the most wonderful mother in all the world, and that they likewise would not trade mothers with anyone.

I do not begrudge anyone his love for his mother; I respect him for it. And once a year all of us observe Mother's Day, all of us together, and we give our mothers gifts, and proudly we take them to our churches and synagogues, and join hands in expressing our love for them.

Even more than this, we learn through our love of our own mother to respect motherhood as such, and we pass laws to protect working mothers, and set up institutions to be motherly to those who have lost their mothers. In short, my love for my mother does not separate me from the sons of other mothers, but brings us all closer together in honoring our mothers.

This is the parable. And its application seems obvious.

I love my mother-faith. I love the ways of prayer that I learned from my parents, the ideals that I absorbed from my religious schoolteachers and my rabbi, I am moved and stirred by the holy days of my religion. I sincerely believe that my mother-faith is the best faith in the world. And I would not trade faiths with any man I know.

And yet, even while loving my mother-faith and believing it to be the finest faith in the world, I know that others love their mother-faith, that they too believe it to be the most wonderful faith in the world and that they likewise would not trade with anyone else.

And I respect their love for their faith. I am taught that respect by our great American tradition. Just as we have tried by law to protect motherhood, so have we by our Constitution protected mother-faiths, and have declared it to be a fundamental right of man that he may live by whatever mother-faith he chooses.

It is in such mutual respect that we must learn to live with good will. Though our mother-faiths differ, though our worship and our theologies vary, we are united on the meaning of justice, we are one on the demands of mercy, we agree on what constitutes a humane and ethical life. In those areas of agreement, there is so much that we can do together, synagogue, church, and cathedral side by side, to bring the message of God's fatherhood and man's brotherhood to our society and to the world.

Let me tell the story of one lad who didn't.

A Jewish boy on the first team of his high school football squad asked to be excused from practice the day before a big game because it was Yom Kippur, the Day of Atonement.

The coach was insistent. "No excuses. We've got a big game coming up. You'll have to be here, Yom Kippur or no Yom Kippur."

"But it's our holiest day of the year, coach. It's like Easter to you. I've just got to be in synagogue."

"Sorry, no excuses. Either come to practice or turn in your uniform."

Sadly the Jewish lad went off to the dressing room to turn in his uniform. But he had been there only a moment when the whole team came piling in. And at their head was a dear friend of his, a Catholic lad, who said to his teammates, "Fellows, this is all wrong. He's not going off some place to have a good time. He's going to pray in his religion, and that's an American right. Fellows, I'm going to turn in my uniform, too!"

At this show of fellowship, the coach changed his mind, and they all played together at the game the day after Yom Kippur.

Somehow the story sings in my heart, because it says so much more than many stories do. It has to do with brotherhood where brothers live. It is not vague or idealistic or off in the clouds; it is where we work and where we play.

Everyone has just such opportunities to demonstrate his convictions as did that Catholic boy. It takes a little imagination and a lot of courage, but all of us who talk of good will can and should also act for good will.

3

Charity Is Justice

In the Hebrew language, justice and charity are linked together. The same word can be used interchangeably for both. The implication is plain: Charity is the justice due to those in need, an obligation upon the giver, a right of the receiver. Therefore, the Bible, while praising the charitable and urging a generous heart, does not leave the needs of the have-nots to the whims of the haves. Charity is commanded by law. The Bible does not say men OUGHT to leave the forgotten sheaf, the corners of the field, the gleanings of the harvest for the poor, the widow, the orphan, and the stranger, but "Thou shalt . . ." It is as though to say that, whether you feel charitable or not, this is a matter of plain justice. "You may not close your hand against your needy brother." The less fortunate were expected to share their meager fare with those in even worse circumstances, and even beggars were expected to give a tithe!

It was of this fundamental obligation of just charity that the very saintly and pious Rabbi Zussya used to preach eloquently and frequently.

One of his congregants, a poor man named Simon, was so moved by Rabbi Zussya's words that he gave a larger-than-tithe-size gift to the rabbi to distribute to the poor. That week, a stroke of good luck came to him and his business improved. Again, after the Sabbath, he gave to Rabbi Zussya's charity fund, and again new customers flocked to his place of business. This went on week after week; Simon would make a large donation, and his business would grow by leaps and bounds, until finally he became quite well-to-do.

Then one day Simon began to calculate. "If," he thought to himself, "my charities through this rather obscure rabbi are so blessed, imagine what would happen if I were to make my gifts through some outstanding teacher of our age." So thinking, that week Simon wrote the famous president of the seminary at which Zussya had been ordained, and made his weekly charity gift through him. That week, one of his best customers canceled a contract. The next week, he sent his check to the seminary head again, and that week two more customers stopped doing business with him. It wasn't long before he was reduced to his original poverty.

Simon finally sought out Rabbi Zussya and confessed everything to him and said, "Tell me why this has happened to me."

"It is simple," Zussya replied. "As long as you gave your charity without calculating whether I was a worthy vessel or not, God was equally generous with you. But when you began to be discriminating, so did God. When you sought worthier distributors of your charity, God sought worthier recipients of His largesse."

Here is a warning against crafty virtue, against calculated charity.

And yet, because we human beings are rational in nature, we want our generosity to make sense. And when our more selfish attributes take the stage and we ask, "Why should we be obligated to charity?" then we might take our cue from a brief Talmudic aphorism: Charity is the salt of money.

To understand this fully, we need only to recall the functions that salt fulfills.

In the first place, salt is a seasoning. It gives flavor to food. If your wife has ever forgotten to put salt into the water in which she boils potatoes, then you know how flat and tasteless a potato can be without it. Salt does not change the flavor, it brings out the flavor. So does money get a flavor from the salt of giving.

When you get a raise in salary, or come into a windfall, what is your first thought? It isn't, now I will have more money, now my bank account will be larger. Unless you are a miser, your first thought is of giving. Now I can give my girl an engagement ring, now I can buy a dishwasher to lighten my wife's load, now I can buy my son a bicycle. The fun of money, the flavor of money, is in what you can do with it to make others happy.

And not only those near and dear to you, but all your fellow men. Certainly in Bible days it must have been a source of real joy for a farmer, after his harvest was gathered, to see the hungry gleaning his fields to keep body and soul together.

And we, whose giving is indirect, going through the channels of social and health and welfare agencies, can derive equal satisfaction and joy from seeing what our gifts have achieved in health, in better homes, and better youngsters, and better cities. This is something that gives flavor to the money in our pocket, something that keeps it from being flat and tasteless. No child can enjoy licking his all-day sucker when a child without one looks on longingly. Instinctively, he knows that charity is the salt of money.

But salt has another function. It is also a preservative. Salted meat will last when fresh meat will spoil. So when we add the salt of charity to our money, we preserve it. Social unrest and social revolution often grow out of hunger. Look to the sources of Fascism in Italy, or Germany, or Japan in the twenties, look to the success of Communism in Russia and in China, and you discover that these movements capitalized on human misery. Great wealth side by side with abject poverty, great wealth which was selfish wealth, which did not recognize that all we have is but lent to us by God, selfish wealth which did not share itself with those in need— the end of that wealth was revolution and death. Those who sought to preserve their wealth by clinging to it, lost it. Had they seasoned it by the salt of generosity, they would have preserved it. We who believe in democracy, in freedom, must preserve that freedom by our voluntary sharing. The best answer to Communism is a socially conscious citizenry who are determined that every man and every child of man shall have the opportunity for guided recreation, for improved health, for better mental attitudes, for wider and deeper and finer living.

Our sages used to say that God determines the annual income of every man, but what he gives away from that income does not diminish it, that God adds to his wealth whatever of it he gives away. Certainly the joy that comes from our income is increased to the extent that we share it. The salt that gives flavor to our wealth and preserves it is our charity.

And we must not forget that charity blends at its edges into justice, that one answer to the need for charity is a greater social justice.

Eight rungs on the ladder of charity

This is the direct implication of the medieval Jewish philosopher Maimonides' eight rungs on the ladder of charity.

"The first and lowest degree is to give, but with reluctance or with regret. This is the gift of the hand but not of the heart.

"The second is to give cheerfully, but not proportionately to need.

"The third is to give cheerfully and proportionately, but not until asked.

"The fourth is to give cheerfully, proportionately, and even unsolicited, but to put it directly into the poor man's hand which shames him.

"The fifth is to give charity in such a way that the distressed may receive the bounty and know their benefactor without their being known to him.

"The sixth, which rises still higher, is to know the objects of our bounty but to remain unknown to them.

"The seventh step is still more meritorious—namely, to bestow charity in such a way that the benefactor may not know the relieved persons, nor they the names of their benefactors, as was done by our fathers during the existence of the Temple. In that holy building was a place called the Chamber of the Silent, where the good left secretly whatever their generous hearts suggested, and from which the poor were maintained with equal secrecy.

"Lastly, the eighth and highest step on the golden ladder of charity is to *anticipate charity by preventing poverty*—to assist a reduced fellow man either by a gift, or loan, or teaching him a trade, or putting him in the way of a job, so that he may earn an honest livelihood and not be forced to the dreadful alternative of holding out his hand for charity."

It is thus that Maimonides precedes by some six hundred years the efforts of modern social agencies and governmental programs that move from charity to justice, from a handout to hand up, and seek, in the establishment of a better society, a more self-reliant, self-supporting, and above all, self-respecting citizenry.

It is this goal which is, or ought to be, at the very heart of religion. The prophets of the Bible united faith and ethics in an indissoluble bond. The essence of piety was its lead-on value to morality. This union of religious observance with social obligation is beautifully illustrated in a story about Israel Salanter, a rabbi of Eastern Europe a century ago.

In modern America, matzoth, the unleavened bread for the Passover, is available on every grocery shelf, and its production has become as mechanized as that of other modern bakery goods.

Not so in the Europe of the nineteenth century. The making of the unleavened cakes, the only wheat product which could be eaten during the Passover week, was a highly complicated process, involving special ovens, special vessels, and the constant supervision of the most expert inspectors.

In the village of Salant, the famous and pious rabbi, Israel Salanter, had for many years supervised the baking of the Passover matzoth. But this year Israel Salanter was sick, and to his bedside there came the elders of the community to seek his advice on preparation for the Passover. "How shall we bake the Passover bread?" they asked. His reply was, "See that the women who do the baking are well paid."

I never hear this story without a tingling at the very roots of my being. For this is in the great prophetic tradition of Isaiah. You can almost hear the elders of ancient Jerusalem asking the prophet, "How shall we fast on the Day of Atonement?" And he answers, "This is the fast that God has ordained, that you feed the hungry and clothe the naked!"

The purpose of religion is righteousness! The purpose of getting right with God is to do right to men! The pieties of the sanctuary are important; we must know how to pray and how to observe the holy occasions, but *only* in order to remind us of the laws of God, the laws of justice, of mercy, and of humility.

How shall we prepare the Passover bread? By paying the baking women well! And how properly worship God? By being just and charitable to those whom He created in His image.

It is your task!

Sometimes a value is best recognized in its absence. We take health for granted until we're sick. So the value of charity and justice are revealed in their absence. When men are not concerned for others, then all society becomes rotten and falls apart.

Nothing in my reading has illustrated this truth more vividly than an incident related by the great trial lawyer and Chief of the War Crimes Trials Section in Germany, Leon

Jaworski, in his book, *After Fifteen Years*. (Gulf Publishing Co., Houston, 1961.)

Some American airmen, shot down over Germany during the Second World War, were transported through the town of Russelsheim, and there, as they marched under guard from one railroad station to another, they were literally beaten to death by a mob of men and women. Years later, the worst offenders were brought to trial; Mr. Jaworski was one of the United States Army attorneys. One witness was called, a minister. He had not taken part in the beatings; he was pious, upright, what we call a good citizen. But he had seen the beatings. He was aware of what was going on.

The lawyer questioned him. "Didn't you undertake to intercede? Didn't you do anything to halt the murders you knew were being committed almost before your very eyes?"

The witness admitted doing nothing.

"Why not? Why could you not attempt to stop it?"

"It was not my task. It was the task of the persons who were leading these prisoners of war to step in for the safety of those prisoners. It was the task of the local police to look out for order in the town. *It was not my task!*"

When you ask, as many have, how could a great nation like Germany have sunk to Hitlerism, you have the answer here. And when you ask how can any city become corrupt, how can any political machine gain control, how can any civilization rot from within, here you have the answer: It is when people, who think of themselves as decent, God-fearing citizens, say, "It is not my task"; it is when good men look on, inactive, at evil, at violence, at dishonesty, at vileness, that the fabric of society begins to unravel.

It is through charity of heart, and justice of law, and above all, the uprightness that underlies them both, that men can best live with their neighbors.

V

Living in Time and Eternity

1

Be Prepared for Leaving

Man, it is said, is the only animal who knows that he will die, and this knowledge colors his whole life. The existentialists of our time make this the key to their whole philosophy, whether that philosophy be religious or atheistic. The inevitability of death and the fear of it, they say, is the mood of all man's thought and striving. If we did not know about death, we would not be driven to think about life and after-life.

It seems to me that the existentialists exaggerate the situation, and it is only natural that they should. Most of them lived through the Second World War in Europe, and walked for years through the valley of the shadow.

But for those of us whose lines are laid in pleasanter places, the knowledge that one day we must die still does affect the way we think, plan, and live. On the one hand, it leads us to value the time we have. And on the other, it compels us to measure our brief years against the longer life of mankind, and the eternity of God.

Children, for whom time stretches out endlessly, who cannot conceive of when they were not here nor when they might no longer exist, build sand castles on the beach and see them washed away by the tide without regret; but the mature will not accept life on those terms, and seek to sculpture enduring monuments that last beyond the tides of time.

Lessons for life must include lessons about death.

Like the child in an amusement park

"So teach us to number our days that we may get us a heart of wisdom," was the prayer of the Biblical Psalmist. But how can a man number his days? The days past, yes, they have a number; but the days that are to come, who knows how many we have?

We are like a child at an amusement park, I once heard a minister say, whose father has given him some money but who is too young to count it. All he knows is how to ask for what he wants and hold out his hand full of coins so that the ticket seller can take the right amount. And so he follows his fancy, eating cotton candy, riding the merry-go-round, buying a pennant, taking a boat ride, until suddenly he looks down at his hand and it is empty. There were other things he meant to buy, other rides he meant to take, but the money is gone, and he sits down and cries.

We are like that child. When we are born, God puts into our hands a certain number of golden hours, and with them we purchase the activities of our lives. At each gate, whether of home, career, or enjoyment, we surrender the hours demanded. And then suddenly we reach into our pockets for more and they are all gone.

We cannot learn to number our days, but we can learn to use them. We may not know how much money we have, but we can learn how much each coin is worth. We may not know when we reach the end of our hours, but we can learn to spend them wisely.

How do you spend your time? Do you waste it? save it? kill it? lose it? use it?

Some people are spendthrifts. Time means nothing to them. They run through it like a four-year-old with a nickel in front of a penny candy counter. The sensation of the moment is all that counts, and who cares about tomorrow?

Some people are misers. They count out the hours as though out of an old-fashioned purse, so deep you can only bring out one coin at a time. They watch the clock at work and they watch the clock at play. They are like a little girl learning to boil eggs who sits and watches each grain of sand drop through the hourglass.

Some people are constantly losing time. Like a watch that runs slowly, they are never on the hour, but always fifteen to thirty minutes late. The only place they will arrive on time is the cemetery. And they miss a lot, like the person on a sight-seeing bus who is so busy looking one way he does not look where the driver is pointing until it's too late.

Others try to save time. What they do with it when they've saved it, I have never quite found out. There's no bank in which you can deposit it for later use. But their life is spent taking "short cuts" to save time.

And some people even kill time, the most tragic murder imaginable. To kill time is like cutting up money with scissors. A man might, as a grandiose gesture, light a cigar with a ten-dollar bill, but at least he ends up smoking. Killing time leaves nothing but trash.

We never have time, except for trouble

One thing is sure about time. We'll always have time for trouble. It's a remarkable thing that we miss so much of life because we're too busy. We haven't time. We keep saying, "If only I had the time, I would do this, read that, go there." But we never have time.

Never, except for trouble, for sickness, for grief.

It really is a pity. I see it over and over again. Children do not have time to visit their parents, men do not have time to take a vacation, people have no time for friendships. But they always have time for trouble.

A businessman I knew never had time to relax. Every time I met him, he would tell me how tired he was, how weary and worn out.

"Why don't you take a vacation?"

"Haven't had a vacation in five years. Haven't the time."

"Then take a long week end. Go fishing, go to a resort."

"Can't do it; can't leave my office. I'm surrounded by incompetents, no one else can take care of it but me."

This was the dialogue almost every time we'd meet. Then, one day in the hospital, his name showed on the register. Heart condition. Now he had lots of time. Twenty-four hours a day. And the office was still open and the business still going. But he had no time to relax, just time to be sick.

I remember another family, a really lovely couple who had moved to our city from out of the state. They used to lament how far away their parents were.

"Why not visit them every six months?" I asked.

"It takes so long. You have to change trains early in the morning."

"Then fly."

"It's too expensive."

And so a year went by, and two. And then they went home to a funeral. They had no time to visit their parents, only time to bury them.

What a distorted sense of time-value we have. We let our lives be run by the clock and the calendar. We have no time to enjoy life, only time to work; no time to be with our loved ones, only time to grieve over them.

How then shall we get us a heart of wisdom? How shall we use our years well?

May I suggest a recipe for the wise use of time? *Plan as though you will live; live as though you will die.* (Like many ideas, I am not sure whether this is my own formulation or one I have heard or read. If it is not original, I give credit to whom it may be due.)

Most of us go to one or the other of these two extremes. Either we worry too much about tomorrow, or spend too much today. Either we live it up, or postpone it too long.

Some folks are worriers. They spend today worrying about tomorrow. They live in the future, talk about the vacation they never take, about what they will do when they are retired. They are concerned about rainy days, they plan without doing, dream without achieving, hope without enjoying. They plan as though they will live, and if ill health or death short-changes them, they are bitter; there was so much they left for later.

Others are the happy-go-luckies who eat, drink, and are merry for tomorrow they die. What they earn, they spend. "Why save?" they ask. "The devil will get it anyhow. Let's live today, let's burn the candle at both ends, because, baby, it's cold outside!" And so, living as though they had only today, their tomorrows are frequently nightmares. The rainy day washes them away.

What we need is a philosophy which combines the best of these. Plan as though you will live, then live as though you will die.

It is not too difficult. All it requires is some thought. First you ask yourself (with pencil in hand), "What is it I want for the rest of my life? Do I have a saving program that will meet the educational needs of our children? Is there something set aside for the days of sickness and tragedy? Will I be able to retire decently? I ought to have a home of my own so that for the monthly payment I will end up with my own cottage. I ought to have a vine and fig tree to sit under when I am sixty so I will plant one now when I am forty. Oh yes, and a hobby. They say that men who quit working and having nothing to replace their work just wither on the vine. I'd better start looking for an outside interest."

This, and a little more of thought and planning to map out the future, set the goals, make up the budget of time and money to meet those goals, and then—your plans made, begin to live, to live as though you will die. Live! Live each moment, each hour, each day as though it were your last on earth. Draw each breath with the same pleasure as that first sniff of fresh air on a nippy fall morning. Look at each tree, each flower, as though it were the first you'd seen and the last you might ever see. Enjoy each moment, each day.

You've no time in such a life for quarrels, for gossip, for nagging, only time for smiles and joy and love.

This is the way to the wise numbering of our years. The large plans are laid, the sensible limits are set to the time and effort and money spent each day, but within those limits, life with joy.

Plan as though you will live, then live as though you will die.

2

Leaving the World a Better Place

And when we die, then what?

Whether we believe in immortality or not (and more of this later), what we are and what we do does live on among men. Our memory persists in those who love us until they, too, are gone. Our influence, our words and our works, live on as long as life is left on earth. Will it or not, we do leave the world a different place. Will it be better for our having lived?

The Talmud underlines this idea with a delightful story. The governor of Judea, Rufus Turnus, passed a yard in which a very old man was planting a carob tree.

"Hey, old fellow," he stopped and called, "do you know how long it takes a carob tree to begin to yield fruit?"

"Seven years, your honor."

"You'll never live to taste it, old man. Why do you waste your time planting it?"

The old gentleman drew himself up with dignity. "When I came into this world, I found carob trees bearing fruit for me to eat. Surely I ought to leave carob trees behind when I die."

Every man who ever cleared a field in the forest, every man who ever dug a drainage ditch in a swamp, every man who ever ploughed a furrow, has left his mark upon the surface of the ground, has left his signature upon nature, has left the world a different place.

So, too, of our mental and spiritual influence. What we say, and what we convey, and what we teach, likewise leaves an imperishable influence upon human life and human history.

This was brought home to me in a most homely and charming way at a meeting of our local Police Association.

A teen-ager was being honored for having saved a little boy from drowning. The Police Association awarded him a watch for his bravery. The youngster was good to look at. He was scrubbed till his face shone, his crew cut stood straight up, and he was properly modest about it all. His parents stood proudly by. But what made the evening memorable were the words of the lad's Red Cross instructor who had been invited to participate.

"I have been an instructor in lifesaving for a long time," he said, "but this is the first time I have known anyone whom I have taught actually to save a life. Now I know what it is like to see work bear fruit."

Those words ought to ring bells in our hearts. There is so much we do the fruit of which we never see. Oh yes, we get a salary for our work, and a thank you (sometimes) for our courtesy, but how many lifesaving instructors see a life saved, and how many teachers see the long-range results of their instruction, and how many preachers know what their words have accomplished, and how many cub scout mothers or boy scout masters see the end product of their hours of labor? Like Johnny Appleseed, we plant and pass on, never returning to see the fruit.

But to know that one Red Cross instructor saw his lifesaving instruction save life, to know that one teacher was remembered by a pupil become great, reassures us of the value of our self-sacrifice.

This same thought is interestingly expressed by Leon Grindon, who wrote: "Nothing so plainly distinguishes between man and brutes as the absolute nothingness of effect in the work of the latter. Unless the Coral Islands be excepted, all the past labors of all the animals that ever existed have left not a trace. These creatures are wise, intense, hardworking, but their work is ephemeral. No law of sequence, perpetuation or accumulation gives unity and permanence to their creations. If all animals were to perish today, nothing of their almost infinite activity would survive."

Of animals, we find only fossil remains. But archeologists find the remnants of whole civilizations, the foundations of houses, tools, pottery.

But there is more here. Men leave their impress not only upon geography but upon the growth of mankind. Every new learned skill, every new resource uncovered, each grass domesticated to grain, each animal made tame, each law of measurement, each principle of sailing, each plot of the stars, has become the possession of mankind. By the spoken word, by the written word, by the legend repeated around the campfire, and by the letter pounded into clay or inked on parchment, the cumulative achievements and lore and knowledge of generation after generation have grown, and mankind is enriched by those whose names are all unknown.

So it is, too, with the values we regard as so self-evident. There are cathedrals in Europe that took centuries to build, but some of the ideas that are the foundation of our lives took millennia in the development. The Bible was more than a thousand years in the writing, and much of what was written in it had been preserved by word of mouth for a thousand years before that. Mankind has hammered out on the anvil of its soul newer and higher revelation of the Almighty. One generation praised His name to another, and added dimensions to divine truth.

We are the heirs of countless millions who laid bricks and wrote books, who planted trees and taught children, who mapped out roads or prophesied new paths. Men leave the world a different place. Will it be better for our having lived?

Let me put the whole matter in another perspective. The Jewish prayer book suggests the figure of a "book of life."

Imagine history as a scroll, that would unroll from eternity to eternity, column after column, beginning with man's first gropings, recording every man's life. Some, like Moses, have left a column, others a sentence, some just their name. Some have left the marks of dirty hands, and some, like Hitler, have smudged whole columns almost beyond reading, but every man has left his name in the book of life. Had Moses not led the people out of Egypt, the book of life would read differently, and had not Reuben, Gad, and Simeon followed Moses out of Egypt, his departure would have left little space in the book. Every one of us is indelibly recorded; our deeds are inscribed in the book of life.

I find myself almost terrified by this picture of human destiny. Hell holds less terror; one takes his chances with God's mercy. But the book of life is written forever. The evil I do may be forgiven me by God, but it cannot be erased from life. Everything you and I say and do becomes part of the future's past. If we teach the saving of life, we may see the fruit of our labors or not, but we have taught it. If we take life, the jury may free us, but the life is taken.

If death is the end, it is the end only of our conscious existence. What we have been and what we have done goes on to bless or to curse the living. To live well is to face the challenge to leave this world a better place for our having been here.

3

Leaving the World a Better Person

We are also challenged, it seems to me, to leave the world a better person. Whatever eternity may be, it begins where life leaves off.

Some years ago, I went to visit an old man in a nursing home. The manager said, before I went into his room, "Rabbi, Mr. G. leaves his light on all day and all night. See if you can persuade him to turn it off."

Entering the room, I could understand why the manager was troubled. This was not a lamp that was left on, but a naked bulb hanging by the wire from the ceiling, swaying in the breeze from the window. It was almost indecently bright, and so, after chatting awhile with Mr. G. I asked him why he burned his light when he was asleep.

His answer was a shocker. "I'll lie in the dark long enough."

Will he? Do we? Is the end of the day just the night, or does the sun rise again?

Almost every known people and every known faith believes in a life beyond the grave. The Greeks left coins with their departed to pay their fare across the river Styx; the Egyptians embalmed their dead so as to last for centuries in physical form; the Indians projected a Happy Hunting Grounds, and the Norsemen a Valhalla.

Is this all a whistling in the dark, a bedtime story to comfort a child afraid of the night? Some say it is. But it is not so easy to dismiss the idea.

From one point of view, immortality might be said to be "proved" by the very universality of man's hunger for and faith in it. By way of analogy we might call attention to a species of fish which live in deep dark caves off the coast of Japan, and in which the eye has atrophied. There being nothing to see, there is no need for anything to see with. Conversely, it might be said, the eye is a response to light. Were there no light, there would never have been a biological eye.

Whence, then, the hunger for life after death if there is no food for that hunger?

And even the skeptics and agnostics who have questioned the idea of immortality and raised questions about it have, when face to face with death, begun to doubt their own doubts. Robert Ingersoll, standing at his brother's graveside, said these words: "Life is a narrow vale between the cold and barren peaks of two eternities. But in the night of death, hope sees a star and listening love can hear the rustle of a wing."

And William James, the proponent of pragmatism, said in his sixties, that he was beginning to think about life after death, and when asked why, replied, "Because I am just becoming fit to live."

John Haynes Holmes, the great New York preacher, regards this statement of James as the clue to an idea which seems to me a very convincing argument for life beyond life.

Man is too richly endowed for a life just on this earth. If this life is all there is, if we are born only to die, then we human beings are given qualities and potentialities for which we have no need. A man does not need music to live; he cannot eat it, it will not keep him warm. Yet music, and the love of music, is a universal human quality. We do not need "true love" to reproduce our kind; passion is enough, yet love rises far beyond the physical and lasts long after the reproductive years. What can explain these and so many other abilities and pursuits of man if this life is all there is?

Nature is very economical. She gives to her children nothing unnecessary. Every physical and mental endowment of a tree, insect, or animal is necessary to that living thing's existence, and nothing more is given. Were human beings designed to live on this earth only, it would have been enough to be endowed with the instincts of an ant. But we have so much more, so much that is unnecessary for a purely biological existence. Why? Did nature suddenly run amok, or has God given us qualities designed to endure beyond the decay of our bodies, qualities that may be superfluous to our physical existence, but useful to the soul's long life? As we grow older we become (or ought to) more fit to live. As our bodies age, our spirits grow toward the life of the spirit that awaits us beyond the grave.

And that life begins where this life leaves off. We start our eternity at whatever point we end our earthly days. From this point of view, our years on earth are a preparation for the world to come. Nor does this downgrade this world any more than describing the college years as years of growth deprives those years of their importance in themselves.

Life is good and is to be lived to the hilt. But we need not leave the light on all night.

Assemble the wardrobe of eternity

The *Zohar*, a medieval mystic commentary on the Bible, puts it in a figure of speech that challenges and inspires.

During its years on earth, the *Zohar* suggests, the soul assembles its wardrobe of eternity, the spiritual garments which it will wear in the next world. Like women who knit, the soul does its own dressmaking and adorns itself with acts of loving-kindness.

It would be interesting, would it not, to see such a garment. Warm love might be its fabric, its buttons pearls of speech; it ought not be cut on any bias, but with straight seams of integrity. It would have no seamy side, nor loose ends, but be whole and holy.

Such garments are not visible. They cannot be worn in any style show, but look deeply into someone's eyes, or watch the play of expression on someone's face, and you can see what sort of garments are being woven by the soul within. Once tailored, they are ours forever; we wear them to eternity. Every sin will be like a patch, every failure a slipped stitch.

I do not know how this idea strikes you, but it disturbs me. If the suit I wear to the office gets threadbare, I give it away and purchase a new one. If my shirt is frayed, I use it for rags and replace it at the store. But my soul's garments are mine forever, and I must tailor them well.

We leave this world. Both what we leave behind and what we take along are permanent, indelibly written in the book of human life, indelibly inscribed in God's Book of Life.

To live, to love, and to leave life with blessing ought to be the goal of every man.